KIDNAPPED TO THE UNDERWORLD

KIDNAPPED TO THE UNDERWORLD

Memories of Xibalba

VÍCTOR MONTEJO

TRANSLATED BY SEAN S. SELL

THE UNIVERSITY OF
ARIZONA PRESS

TUCSON

The University of Arizona Press
www.uapress.arizona.edu

We respectfully acknowledge the University of Arizona is on the land and territories of Indigenous peoples. Today, Arizona is home to twenty-two federally recognized tribes, with Tucson being home to the O'odham and the Yaqui. Committed to diversity and inclusion, the University strives to build sustainable relationships with sovereign Native Nations and Indigenous communities through education offerings, partnerships, and community service.

ISBN-13: 978-0-8165-5259-7 (paperback)
ISBN-13: 978-0-8165-5260-3 (ebook)

Cover design by Leigh McDonald
Cover art adapted from *Owls in a Mountain Gorge* by Alexandre Calame, courtesy of the Finnish National Gallery
Designed and typeset by Leigh McDonald in 10.5/14 Electra LT Std and Ive WF (display)

Publication of this book is made possible in part by the proceeds of a permanent endowment created with the assistance of a Challenge Grant from the National Endowment for the Humanities, a federal agency.

Library of Congress Cataloging-in-Publication Data
Names: Montejo, Víctor, 1951– author. | Sell, Sean S., translator.
Title: Kidnapped to the underworld : memories of Xibalba / Víctor Montejo ; translated by Sean S. Sell.
Other titles: Sun tracks ; v. 95.
Description: Tucson : University of Arizona Press, 2024. | Series: Sun tracks : an American Indian literary series ; volume 95
Identifiers: LCCN 2023037905 (print) | LCCN 2023037906 (ebook) | ISBN 9780816552597 (paperback) | ISBN 9780816552603 (ebook)
Subjects: LCSH: Mayas—Guatemala—Folklore. | Voyages to the otherworld—Folklore.
Classification: LCC PQ7499.2.M66 K5313 2024 (print) | LCC PQ7499.2.M66 (ebook) | DDC 863/.64—dc23/eng/20240202
LC record available at https://lccn.loc.gov/2023037905
LC ebook record available at https://lccn.loc.gov/2023037906

Printed in the United States of America
♾ This paper meets the requirements of ANSI/NISO Z39.48-1992 (Permanence of Paper).

To my parents and grandparents
Eusebio Montejo and Juana Esteban Méndez,
Antonio Esteban and Candelaria Méndez
that in peace they may rest with my ancestors
under the shade of the great tree of life
there in kamb'al, the place of death,
away from pain, colds, and the coronavirus.

Thanks to
the Middle American Research Institute (MARI),
Tulane University, Louisiana, for allowing me
to use the photos of Oliver La Farge that show
the pueblo of Jacaltenango during the 1920s.

MAP 1 Map of Guatemala. Jacaltenango, located near the Guatemala-Mexico border.

CONTENTS

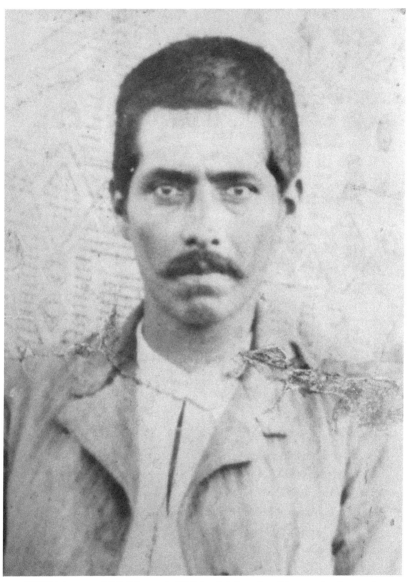

FIGURE 1 Antonyo Mekel Lawuxh. This book is based on his near-death experience. Photo by Antonio Esteban, 1920.

PREFACE

THE HISTORY of the world is cyclical. The twenty-first century has arrived, saddled with the pain and suffering our grandparents endured in the past. Each generation has suffered more than the next, beginning with the Spanish invasion in 1524, colonization and encomiendas (1540–1791), forced labor on plantations, and the construction of roads and highways before and after the so-called Independence of Guatemala (1795–1821). In addition, the Armed Conflict during the second half of the twentieth century (1960–1996) dropped its weight on Indigenous communities with massacres and scorched earth military tactics. Consequently, the invaders brought: wars, pandemics, exploitation, kidnappings and genocide, events that have left an indelible mark on the minds and hearts of the Indigenous inhabitants of the Mayab'.

The Indigenous worldview and our beliefs in a life beyond death have changed dramatically, although at times disguised behind the Christian tradition that in many ways it resembled. For the Maya, dying was only a change of state in which one leaves the body on earth and the soul begins a journey full of obstacles to reach eternal rest in *kamb'al*, the Place of Death. There, those who did good by serving their people, honoring God, and protecting nature came to rest without many obstacles under the shade of the great tree of life. In that place there was everything. It simulated the life and activities that people had done on earth. The difference was that, in this place of eternal rest, the good did not suffer, not even colds, as mentioned in this work. On the other hand, the bad were astray from the road, because they could not pass the obstacles, and in this way they continued to suffer, lost forever.

According to Maya belief, the dead return every year during the feast of All Saints' Day (November 2) to reunite with their loved ones still here on earth. In turn, these living relatives must offer them food, fruits, candles, and flowers so that, with their aroma, they can nourish their spirit.

With the imposition of Christianity, the vision of the world and the beyond of Indigenous peoples changed, and with it, the meaning of death. Now they had to pray and go to churches, work on building temples, and pay tithes and tributes to achieve heaven and eternal bliss. With this came the fear of hell, or the eternal fire trumpeted by the churches, where the devil, a character with a tail and horns, waited with a trident for the damned.

In the violent encounter of these two worlds, the Indians realized that the actions of the invaders and missionaries were not what they preached. How much terror they caused in the populations! These "Christians" hanged the Indigenous leaders and Maya sages, bearers of the ancestral tradition. As a consequence of this fear and terror implemented by the invaders, the people took refuge behind the Catholic religion, while secretly maintaining their values and knowledge inherited from the ancient Maya. So the inhabitants were not easily assimilated, and their traditions were written and kept in secret places, such as the case of the *Popol Vuh*, which was found and translated by the friar Francisco Ximénez at the end of the eighteenth century.

The *Popol Vuh* was a pan-Maya book, and the creation myths and other traditions it related were still repeated in the oral tradition of the Maya people of Guatemala. The idea of the existence of the underworld, where souls will rest after passing the trials on their way, was repeated from generation to generation, although not exactly as it appears in the original text of the *Popol Vuh*. Thus, the twin heroes, Hunahpú and Ixbalanqué, the two who managed to defeat in the ball game the lords of Xiwb'alb'a, the Place of Fear, went and returned, having overcome all the tests on their way. So, after fulfilling their mission, Hunahpú rose to the sky and became the sun, while his companion Ixbalanqué became the moon.

There is no doubt that the stories of trips to the beyond, "to the region of death," as related by the *Popol Vuh*, have a pre-Hispanic origin, and that they continued in the oral tradition after the Maya books, such as the original of the *Popol Vuh*, were hidden to avoid being destroyed or burned by the early missionaries. With the arrival of the Catholic religion, medieval images and representations of heaven and hell were integrated into Indigenous beliefs, forming a syncretic tradition between the Maya and the Christian religion.

The Maya believe that death sometimes comes prematurely when certain lost spirits kidnap their victims and forcibly take them to the Place of Death. This explains why many times people relive and tell their experiences in the afterlife, a process that is known as near-death experience.

The same thing happened during the armed conflict in Guatemala, when many Indigenous people and peasants were kidnapped and forcibly taken to the Place of Death (military detachments), where they were dismembered. Very few managed to escape this Place of Death and tell their stories of pain and suffering caused by these evil lords, who still continue to oppress the Indigenous peoples of Guatemala. Many mothers now, like grandmother Ixmucané, are waiting for the return of their children who disappeared during the armed conflict that took place between the Guatemalan army and the guerrillas of the United Guatemalan National Revolutionary Front (URNG). The bones of those loved ones still complain in mass graves, struggling to recompose their bodies and emerge into a world of light and peace, as Hunahpú and Ixbalanqué did when they emerged from Xiwb'alb'a according to the *Popol Vuh*.

HOW THIS STORY WAS WRITTEN

During my vacation at the Santiago Indigenous Institute for Boys in Antigua Guatemala in 1971, and a year away from graduating as an elementary school teacher, I asked my mother about a story she had told me a long time ago, when I was a child. It was about my grandfather, who had had a near-death experience. She told me that my grandfather was in bed for several years, until one day he died. Then, my mom told us that, after being dead for several hours, my grandfather came back to life. And when he was better, he told the family what he had seen there in *kamb'al*, the Place of Death.

I asked my mother to sit down and tell me the story more slowly, because I wanted to take notes. She told me the story again, but she had forgotten some passages that she told me some twelve years earlier, which I kept vaguely in my memory.

According to my mother, my grandfather knew Spanish and had served the town in many ways, but at that time people wanted him to accept this important position as *alkal txah*, or prayer-maker. In this sacred service, a person had to devote himself full time to serving God and the people, while putting aside his own works. The position lasted a year, during which time the prayer maker was dedicated to organizing community works, prayers, and ceremonies according to the ancient Maya calendar. My mother said that my grandfather refused, saying he had already served and that was why he was very poor. It was time for them to look for someone else and leave him alone. My grandfather was right, because those who served in this sacred "office" ended up being very poor and their families suffered the consequences.

But it was also a big problem if service to God and the people was rejected. He who disobeyed or rejected the service to which he was called was practically rejecting his own health and the blessings of the Creator. According to the ancient tradition of the people, to refuse sacred service was to condemn oneself to suffering and pain. The elders, or principales, reminded my grandfather of the consequences of refusing the service, but he kept refusing. Obviously, my grandfather was also unsure because he had noticed how the parish priest and the Ladino civil authorities had persecuted the traditional Maya authorities in the past.

My grandfather had been ill for several years. Even so, sick and struggling, he worked in the small milpa that he had managed to sow. Surely, my mother said, he was no longer the same strong man as before, who had proudly lifted the spirit of the people. According to the *ahb'eh*, or diviners, who had come to see him, he had broken the thread of tradition, and therefore the whole family suffered from extreme poverty, because he had become very weak in health. One afternoon, while my grandfather was cleaning the milpa, that strange disease affected him strongly. My grandfather came to the house saying he had had a disturbance in the milpa. He said some seedlings on the banks of the milpa and under some rocks had mocked him, saying: "*Antonyo Mekel Lawuxh, nab'nhe-tik'a chach munlayi, matoj aytik'a tzet cha'a' tawet. Suktaj sk'ul! Ha ha ha . . .* ! (Antonio Mekel Lawuxh, it is useless for you to keep working because you will not achieve anything! Fool, ha ha ha . . . !")

My mother clearly remembered that moment when my grandfather seemed crazy. Even though my grandmother, Candelaria Méndez, called the best healers in town, no one knew what was happening to Grandfather. Everyone believed he was paying for his sin for having rejected the sacred traditions of the people. After several weeks, my grandfather came back to his senses, but couldn't get up from his bed. It was in these conditions that he had that dream, vision, or near-death experience that my mother retold me.

As a student, my first impulse was to read the great Maya book, the *Popol Vuh*, to try and understand. Then I read other major literary works, such as El Señor Presidente, and Hombres de Maíz, by Miguel Ángel Asturias, *Don Quixote de la Mancha*, by Cervantes, and the *Divine Comedy*, by Dante Alighieri. I realized that my grandfather's dream or vision was somewhat like *Popol Vuh* and the *Divine Comedy*, so I decided to document the story that my mother kept in her memory and that she had repeated and transmitted to me orally. Prepared then with paper and pencil, I asked my mother to sit down and tell me Grandpa's story again, sometimes helping her remember some details she was forgetting. I wanted to write the story because I had had a dream, to be a writer, and this would be my first book. My mother said that Grandpa insisted until the day of his death, that he had been kidnapped from beyond the grave, but that he had come back to life to testify to what he had gone to see there in the afterlife. My mother agreed, and for several afternoons she told these stories that as a child had caused me a lot of fear. She told me fragments of the story in our Maya language, Popb'alti', and I wrote it directly into Spanish. In my autobiography, Entre dos Mundos: Una Memoria (Editorial Piedra Santa, 2021), I refer to how this manuscript was written.

According to my mom, my grandfather was aggravated by the disease and one afternoon he stopped breathing and died. My grandmother and her neighbors started crying out loudly as was customary in the village when someone died. People from the community began to arrive to accompany them during the wake. Grandfather was dead for several hours and people prayed the rosary to start the novena for the eternal rest of his soul. Then, the inexplicable happened. As the relatives of the dead man prepared the corpse for burial, people were shocked to see that the body began to move. Grandpa began to breathe, and gradually sat on the edge of the table where he had been laid, covered with a white blanket. He had come back to life, but he could not speak in those moments.

Three days passed before he started talking. The first thing he did was call his daughters and other relatives to tell them about his experience in the afterlife. Grandpa exhorted: *There is indeed another life beyond this one that we live here on Earth. There are also punishments for those who disobey the laws of God and nature.* The grandfather recounted his journey to *kamb'al*, or the Place of Death, where he was taken by two guides and protectors to see the sufferings in the underworld. Something like when the poet Virgil rescued Dante in the Valley of Pain and led him as a good guide to the eternal realms of suffering and saved souls, according to the *Divine Comedy*.

I was fortunate to be interested at an early age in the values of oral tradition, language, and culture of my people. At that time, the Maya culture was deteriorating and being lost, as the bearers of the culture were insulted and discriminated against as "Indians." I questioned myself about the validity or viability of my parents' and grandparents' Maya culture. Would it be good enough as a source of inspiration and literary writing? I even wondered if an Indigenous Maya could dream of being a writer. That's what I thought as I read and began to gather my ideas to write my first manuscript.

I had my notes, the ones I had written during the holidays, and finally I started restructuring the manuscript and recreating my grandfather's vision. Sometimes I felt a strange sensation of fear, because I was reviving his story as if I were in his shoes. Every afternoon and after school, I dedicated myself to writing this history, giving it the literary touch according to my imagination in the context of the Maya culture. As the poet I wanted to be, I would have to create and recreate that story of which my mother only remembered fragments, but with my ability to weave stories I was able to give life and unity to the text. Unfortunately, I didn't have a typewriter, nor were there computers back then, so I started writing my novel by hand. Then, I used a machine from the institute to polish what I had written several times by hand. In other words, this was my beginning as a writer, because I simply

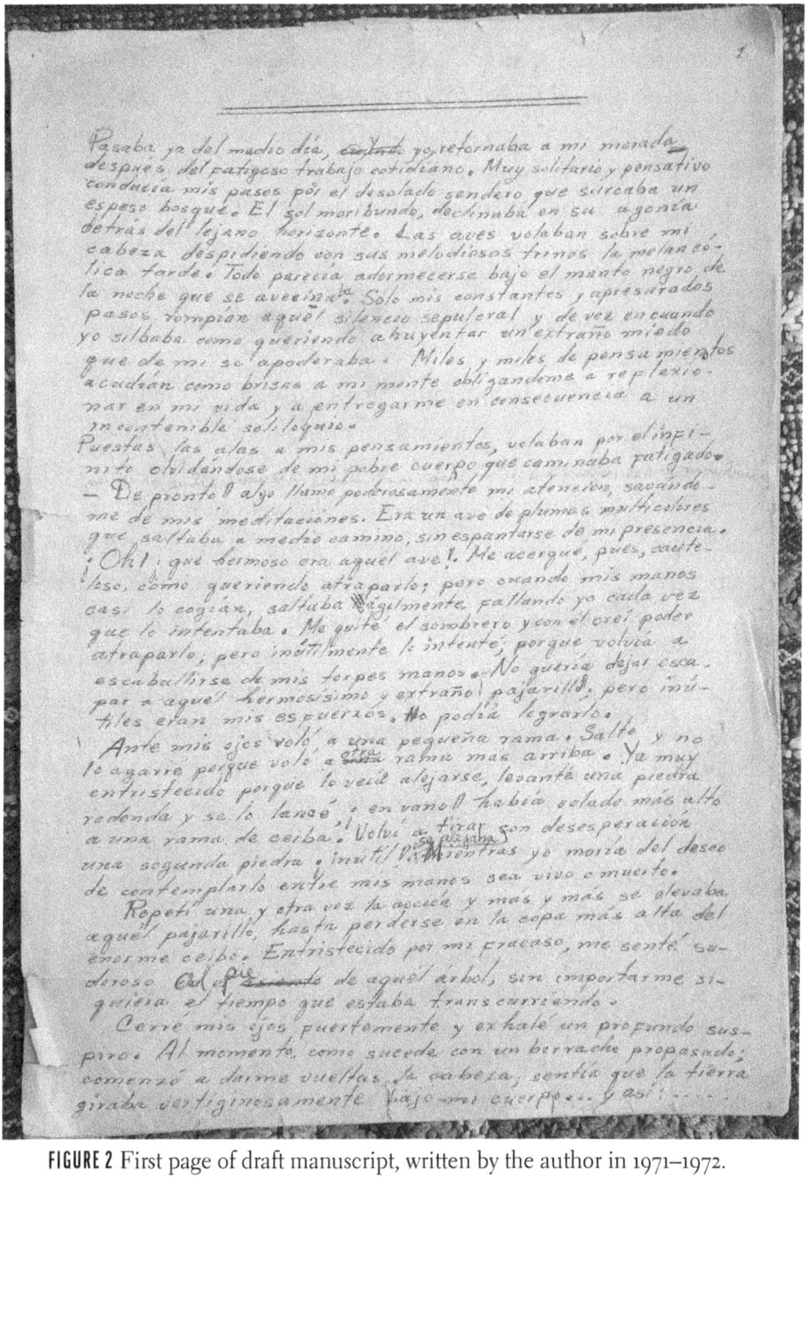

Pasaba ya del medio día, ~~cuando~~ yo, retornaba a mi morada después del fatigoso trabajo cotidiano. Muy solitario y pensativo conducía mis pasos por el desolado sendero que surcaba un espeso bosque. El sol moribundo, declinaba en su agonía detrás del lejano horizonte. Las aves volaban sobre mi cabeza despidiendo con sus melodiosos trinos la melancólica tarde. Todo parecía adormecerse bajo el manto negro de la noche que se avecinaba. Solo mis constantes y apresurados pasos rompían aquel silencio sepulcral y de vez en cuando yo silbaba como queriendo ahuyentar un extraño miedo que de mí se apoderaba. Miles y miles de pensamientos acudían como brisa a mi mente obligándome a reflexionar en mi vida y a entregarme en consecuencia a un incontenible soliloquio.

Puestas las alas a mis pensamientos, volaban por el infinito olvidándose de mi pobre cuerpo que caminaba fatigado.
— De pronto algo llamó poderosamente mi atención, sacudiéndome de mis meditaciones. Era un ave de plumas multicolores que saltaba a medio camino, sin espantarse de mi presencia. ¡Oh! qué hermoso era aquel ave!. Me acerqué, pues, cauteloso, cómo queriendo atraparlo; pero cuando mis manos casi lo cogían, saltaba ágilmente, fallando yo cada vez que lo intentaba. Me quité el sombrero y con él creí poder atraparlo, pero inútilmente lo intenté, porque volvía a escabullirse de mis torpes manos. No quería dejar escapar a aquel hermosísimo y extraño pajarillo, pero inútiles eran mis esfuerzos. No podía lograrlo.

Ante mis ojos voló a una pequeña rama. Salté y no lo agarré porque voló a otra rama más arriba. Ya muy entristecido porque lo veía alejarse, levanté una piedra redonda y se lo lancé, en vano! había volado más alto a una rama de ceiba. Volví a tirar con desesperación una segunda piedra. inútil!. Mientras yo moría del deseo de contemplarlo entre mis manos sea vivo o muerto.

Repetí una y otra vez la acción y más y más se elevaba aquel pajarillo, hasta perderse en la copa más alta del enorme ceibo. Entristecido por mi fracaso, me senté sudoroso ~~al pie~~ de aquel árbol, sin importarme siquiera el tiempo que estaba transcurriendo.

Cerré mis ojos fuertemente y exhalé un profundo suspiro. Al momento, como sucede con un borracho propasado, comenzó a darme vueltas la cabeza, sentía que la tierra giraba vertiginosamente bajo mi cuerpo... y así...

FIGURE 2 First page of draft manuscript, written by the author in 1971–1972.

had the desire to recreate and expand those stories and seek their publication, trying to make that dream I had as a child come true, when I envisioned many books inscribed with my name, Victor Montejo, as the author.

When I finished the manuscript, I took it to my literature teacher. I told him that the document was a recreation of my grandfather's story. After reading it, my teacher, Reverend Brother Sebastián Farró Soler (RIP), told me that it was a very interesting story and that it was worth seeking publication. I remember him telling me: *The novel is very interesting, but it has many sections of Hinduism.* I explained to my teacher that the stories had been told to me by my mother in the Maya language. Therefore, as an illiterate Maya woman, she knew nothing of Hinduism. My teacher insisted: *Dear son, you are a Catholic and a good Christian, so we must eliminate those sections that are passages of Hinduism.* The professor crossed out those sections and I removed them. I no longer remember the passages I deleted, but when the manuscript was ready, I handed it back to him.

Brother Sebastian said he would take me to Ciudad Vieja, near Antigua Guatemala, where there was a printing press that could publish this manuscript that we titled *Kidnapped to the Underworld*. Arriving in Ciudad Vieja, we entered the convent of a church, and there we spoke with the priest and director of the printing press. We left the manuscript for the editor and publisher to read.

After several weeks, the professor accompanied me to ask whether they had decided to publish the work. The priest and editor handed me the novel saying: *The novel is very interesting and could be published, but you would have to pay two hundred quetzales for its publication. You are not a known author and there is no assurance that we can sell many copies of this novel.* When the publisher said I should pay that sum of money, my hopes of being a writer vanished. I was just a scholarship boy and I had never had more than twenty quetzals at a time in my hands; how could I gather two hundred quetzals and pay for the publication of my book? So, I thought that writing and publishing books was something that only rich people could do.

Very sad, I went back to school and kept the manuscript in a box under my bed. I suppressed my impulses to be a writer. Although the novel was not published, my mother was happy that I had written it, because according to her, my grandfather had insisted that the message had to be passed on to people who wanted to listen. She has always believed that there really is an afterlife where people pay for their sins committed on earth. My mother constantly told her children what Grandpa told her that day of his trip to the afterlife in order to teach us respect for life, evade vices, and prepare us to be good children of town. Possibly, my mother would have totally forgotten this story if Grandfather did not insist, shortly before he died, that she must relay it to her children. All this was possible because of my desire to write it and recreate the story of what my mother remembered about that distant event.

I kept the manuscript in a chest and kept writing myths and other stories, because I didn't want to give up.

Years passed and 1982 arrived, when the armed conflict intensified in Guatemala. Unfortunately, the Indigenous populations were attacked by the army as a way of controlling the guerrilla movement, which, according to the army and the Guatemalan elite, was supported by the Indigenous people. I had to go into exile to the United States in November of 1982 and leave my manuscripts behind, thinking I would soon return to my village. Two years after my absence, the manuscript was rescued by my wife when she left the country with my children; mice had begun to gnaw the pages. Other manuscripts had been buried, and after two decades in exile it was impossible to rescue them.

On different occasions, I worked on the manuscript, trying to polish the story for publication. First, I started it as a story being recounted by a third person, my grandfather, but then I found that I was already writing in first person, as if my grandfather was personified in me. In this way, it was easier for me to construct the story, as I felt the sense of fear and awe about death and the afterlife, as if I were the actor in this novel. Unfortunately, my mother became ill for many years, so I put the manuscript aside, not wanting to think about death and the afterlife. Five years ago, my mother passed away, and I felt the need, once again, to retake the project of editing and preparing the text for publication. The following is the result of that effort.

KIDNAPPED TO THE UNDERWORLD

1

CONFUSION

I WAS already late as I was coming back from working in the milpa that day. Though I knew the way to my pueblo very well, I suddenly found myself lost in the thick woods, unsure where I was going. The solitude took my heart prisoner, and I grew sad thinking that no one accompanied me on that grim and desolate path. Oh, how terrible is solitude! I walked and walked with no one to give me directions or point the correct way home. Time passed, bit by bit, and I began to lose hope. Father Sun was dying, and night darkened the peaks of the far-off mountains.

The birds in the forest started flying like crazy, their melodious trills bidding farewell to the melancholy afternoon. Everything seemed to be falling asleep under the looming black cloak of night. Only my constant and hurried steps broke that sepulchral silence, and from time to time I whistled, hoping it could help me escape the overpowering fear. Thousands of thoughts pecked at my brain like a crazed woodpecker, forcing me to reflect on my past life. And so, pensive and sweaty, I gave myself over into an uncontainable soliloquy.

My thoughts took wing, flying to the infinite, forgetting my poor body that walked fatigued within that shadow of chilling monotony. Soon something called powerfully to my attention, shaking me from my meditations. It was a bird of many-colored feathers that hopped in the middle of the path, not a bit disturbed by my presence. Oh, how beautiful was that bird!

I approached cautiously, hoping to catch it, but just when my hands almost had it, the bird would jump nimbly from the ground, making me fail each time. I took off my hat in hopes of using it to catch the bird, but again it scurried away from my clumsy hands. Ah, I didn't want to let that most beautiful and strangely colored fowl get away, but my efforts kept proving futile.

Before my eyes the bird arose and flew to a small branch, nearly within my reach. I jumped as high as I could, but I couldn't grasp it because it flew to a higher branch. Now very desperate, I picked up a round stone and rashly threw it. In vain! The bird had flown higher, to a ceiba branch. Frantically, I hurled a second stone, but the extraordinary bird kept ascending and going further away. Meanwhile, I was dying from the intense desire to contemplate and caress it between my hands. I kept throwing my hopeless stones, but the colorful bird continued until it was lost in the topmost canopy of the enormous ceiba.

It was as if that multicolored bird had guided me to the highest elevations, toward a higher goal that I would have to reach, but which would require much more effort. Saddened by my failure, I sat down, sweaty, at the foot of that tree without even caring about the time passing by. I felt so sad, as if I had just lost the most valuable treasure, or as one who loses part of their own being.

Weariness finally took me over, and I decided to lie down on the ground and rest. But as I was doing that, my head started spinning like I was drunk. Then the earth seemed to move dizzily from under my feet, and I collapsed on the ground, losing consciousness.

Suddenly I was in great danger, as I somehow found myself attached to the roots and vines growing on the wall of a great abyss.

Poor me! There I was, clinging helplessly to the rock like a climber stuck on that vertical wall. I had managed to reach the middle of the abyss when I began to lose strength and give up. From below, I heard the frightening rumble of a prodigious river running precipitously through gigantic rocks. Over my head rose the vertical side of the ravine, impossible to climb.

I couldn't even take another step, I was stuck, holding onto those fragile roots to keep from falling into the precipice. One false step meant certain death. Who could save me if there was no one with me? To whom could I scream? Where could I direct my voice if no one could hear me? Never in my life have I felt so alone and wretched as I found myself in those moments. But I had one hope; and therefore, I made a great effort to maintain my balance. More than anything, I had the desire to keep living and return to my pueblo with my family.

There I was, fighting desperately against the death that was stalking me, when I was amazed to see a ball of fire come falling from the sky to strike my trembling chest. That unbelievable light strengthened my body and infused me with tremendous valor. In this way I felt myself a man full of bravery and with new hopes to keep living. Then, with utmost care I began the dangerous ascent, holding tightly to those tenuous roots in the vertical wall of that overwhelming precipice. Great was my astonishment when I found I had reached the top of the abyss and could finally move unscathed from that immense danger.

I don't know how I happened to expose my life to the middle of that great precipice, nor did I see the benevolent hand that rescued me from such horrible risk, placing me on the most accessible path.

Tired and dazed, I lay down at the foot of some old guava trees. The afternoon continued on its sad way, grey and unforgettable, and the clouds rolled apart and back together, forming strange figures that found no exit from the sky. There was sun, but it was a pale sun whose rays brought no heat.

There I stayed, quietly contemplating the grey and nebulous sky. I was so engrossed that I failed to dodge the droppings a damned vulture left on my head. At that precise moment also a husky-voiced owl began to sing, sometimes sounding like the cackle of the very devil, laughing at my lamentable situation. That owl was the messenger of the lords from beyond, and its song sounded to me like the funeral chimes that tolled when they buried someone in my pueblo.

So funereal was the owl's song that my heart began to race from fear and anguish of being there alone. Everything in my surroundings started to laugh at me. Even some mushrooms from a rock signaled, shouting, "Bad job, *tatita*, no matter how much you work, you won't achieve anything. Fool, foooool! Ha ha ha haaaa!"

Those insults were unbearable, and so I ran like crazy to pull out those accursed plants that provoked my terrible wrath. Ah, *carajo*! Tiny creatures were insulting me. In truth I felt so alone and totally abandoned.

I sat down again, and this time the infernal noises departed, leaving me a brief respite. All those evil omens scared me, for they were the heralds of the same death that pursued me. Confused and exhausted, I stayed sitting on the edge of the ravine, contemplating at the same time the querulous nature that surrounded me.

2

THE ABDUCTION

STILL WEAK, weary, and mournful, I sat under the shadow of those guava trees, when suddenly there appeared before my eyes an unknown man, his skin as pale as paper. Never had I seen such a strange and pallid man as this, as if no blood ran through his veins.

The dread that infused me proclaimed that it was not a living being, but rather a spirit, a soul, or someone from the realm of death. His presence left me entirely dazed, unable to scream or say a single word. Meanwhile, this strange character fixed his eyes on me and was approaching like an automaton where I was sitting. My body was paralyzed, and I could neither react nor defend myself. I wanted to ask who he was, what his name was, and why he was chasing me, but the words would not come from my mouth. So terrified was I that I could barely make even the faintest sounds, which made me feel I'd been rendered speechless.

When he came to my side, he brusquely took my hand and pulled me to my feet while he ordered me in a hoarse and imperious voice: "Come, I will lead you!"

When I heard that voice from beyond the grave, sounding like a radio with dying batteries, and when I felt that cold, skeletal hand like ice touching mine, my knees buckled, and I fell flat on my face. There I stayed, and all I could do was listen, because I lost all notion of time, the world, and everything that exists on earth. Surely I was now in an unknown, liminal world, between life and death. Overwhelmed by this mysterious journey, I was soon transported, like a bird in swift flight, to that supernatural world invisible to human eyes.

How did I arrive at that strange place? I don't know, for I was like one who has been kidnapped and driven blindfolded and who, on his return, does not even know where he has gone. Thus was I, oblivious to everything; my memory and thoughts no longer with me. An influx of dim light, a mysterious breath, guided and governed me. Beyond the slightest doubt, I no longer belonged to the world of mortals, but had come to be an inhabitant of the "second life."

Suddenly, the one who had snatched me from the living and I found ourselves in the middle of a wide, completely cleared path on a strange new road passing through the middle of an immense plain of dry grass. The panorama, I saw, was somewhat like that of earth, but also indescribably different, due to the pallor and coldness of the terrain.

The mysterious man was leading me hastily, trying to move me off the true path as quickly as possible. He pulled me and pushed me and insisted I follow him quickly, as if afraid that someone would discover him dragging me against my will.

So, I was anxious to follow him quickly when, far down the wide road, I saw a dust cloud rising from something or someone approaching quickly towards us. Then the one leading me, seeing someone galloping up to block his way, stopped abruptly, proffering curses. I was confused, not understanding why the man was so busy dragging me who knows where. Seeing that this strange man wanted to hide from the one galloping near, I also tried to resist, to avoid being kidnapped.

But in a short time, the horseman reached us. He was dressed all in white and mounted on a horse also white. He immediately dismounted and intercepted the strange man who was driving me wildly.

"Oh, fool! How dare you snatch this poor man before his time?" The newcomer said to my captor, at the same time taking my hand.

"He's mine, this man belongs to me!" the pale-skinned one who was driving me responded with fury.

My protector tried to make this strange man see that he had snatched me before my time and that I did not belong to him, but the one with the pale face kept insisting that I did. Then my defender, to end the argument, made a proposal.

"Let him lie on the ground. After he is stretched out and rigid, try to lift him in your arms. If you manage to lift him from the ground, then he will be yours; but if not, you should leave him alone and not disturb him again."

And so it was done. I lay down on the hard ground like someone who wants to take in the sun, and I stayed there firm and still. Then the man who sought to seize me stepped forward and tried to lift me as he had been ordered. But, to my surprise, that man did not manage to get me up a centimeter above the ground. Enraged, he struggled with me, but as much as he fought, he could not move me from the ground. It was as if a child were trying to lift up a horse. Mysteriously my body began to feel like a bag full of lead. Seeing that he could not lift me, the man stepped aside, and then my liberator picked me up without the slightest difficulty. He lifted me off the ground like a child, and with just one hand he spun me in the air several times, demonstrating his power. The attacker was surprised and no longer tried anything else, but withdrew with his tail between his legs, furious and totally defeated.

Ah! How calm I felt when I saw him walking away, leaving me alone. At the same time, I felt happy to see that someone cared for me, and I no longer felt totally helpless.

When my protector saw that man walking away like an injured dog, he raised his sword straight up to the sky, as if making a sign. At that moment, and in compliance with that order or signal, another man dressed in white descended from that level of the sky to the place where we were. Then, the rider who had rescued me spoke to the one who had come down from that cloudy sky.

"This man," he said, pointing to me, "was brought early and has to return to the place of the living. But since he is already here in the *kamb'al* or place of death, it is convenient that he witnesses some of the sufferings in the mansion of Vukub' Q'aquix, the Seven Fires or Lucifer. Take him to the next level, to the main door, and there you will learn what you must do from those who manage that place."

This is what he said, and then he again mounted his shining steed and rode off to the place from whence he had appeared. My new companion smiled kindly and took me by the arms to lead me to the door where the dead arrive. Now I realized that the one who had abducted me wanted to lead me on a false path to deceive me. According to my protectors, I was not yet dead, but my spirit was lost in that liminal world, between life and death.

We walked a short time, then we arrived at a huge, closed door which had several iron locks. This black door was enormous and seemed impossible to open with only the force of man. We stopped at the door and my companion told me:

"Kneel down, kneel down! You must pronounce here some of the prayers that you used to pray back on earth to open this door. Only with prayers can this huge door be opened," insisted my guide.

I stayed pensive a long time, because it was difficult to remember the prayers that I prayed most when I was on earth. It was strange, here I no longer ruled my own being, for I was beginning to lose my memory of earthly things.

After a brief moment of meditation, I began to say an Our Father, the Act of Contrition, and a Hail Mary.

After I had finished saying these prayers, my guide asked: "Who is Hunab' K'uh?"

"Hunab' K'uh is the One True God, the Creator of heaven and earth. He is lord of life and movement, Komam Jahaw, whom we should thank now and forever, and in every place," I replied, a bit more serene.

Then he asked me, "How does Hunab' K'uh manifest?"

"Hunab' K'uh manifests in the sky-lightning, the lightning bolt, and the thunder. These three forces are those that represent Hunab' K'uh; the same way The Holy Trinity is the union of the Father, the Son and the Holy Spirit," I responded according to what I had learned from the holy book of our ancestors, the *Popb'al Hum.*

When I finished saying these words, the great door opened as if it were a simple sheet of paper moved by a strong wind.

"Now we enter!" said my guide, and so he took me to the presence of the man who seemed to be the master of that room.

This place looked like a secretarial office, as several men were writing at tables. I also saw on the tables many huge books with black printing. It seemed like I had arrived at the municipal court in my town where the Ladino clerks handle large and voluminous books of baptisms and deaths.

I fell to my knees before them, and the master took me by the hand.

"Arise! We will examine your body to see which path you must follow."

With much fear and timidity, I followed those bewildering orders. I was still wondering, how could I have arrived in this mysterious place?

So, that strange personage proceeded to examine my body as doctors and healers do when they want to detect the evil that afflicts a patient. The man examined my eyes and ears and then pulled my tongue to watch me carefully.

"Very good," he concluded. "Extend your hands now," he told me, and I did.

He meticulously checked the palms of my hands as if he were looking for some information imbued there. And as this strange doctor finished examining my body and the senses that, I think, were more relevant here, he diagnosed me by saying:

"How could you come here if your hour has not yet come? So you may understand," he told me, "here is the list of those who have to come this year, and your name does not appear among them."

The list was tremendously long, comprising thousands and thousands of names of people from different parts of the world who would have to leave the land that year because of death. It might be from famines, suicides, homicides, wars, plagues, earthquakes, or accidents.

The guardian of that room also brought to my attention a large black book, still sealed with gold ribbons. This was the book of life, he told me. After quickly reviewing the pages of this great book, he said, "There are still many sheets of this book to be turned until your name appears, and you are called. You have, then, many more years of life, and you will see your children grow and serve your people."

After listening carefully to his words, I said, trembling, "I, Lord, do not know how I came here, and I do not even know where I am; but if I am granted the grace to return to my small town, I am ready to return right now."

Then, that man in charge of the books told his assistants, "Call Mekel Lawuxh to talk to our visitor."

Two of the man's assistants left immediately to call my father, who had died some years ago. A short time later they arrived bringing my father.

"Who is this?" they said, pointing at me.

"Oh, it's my son Antonio!" said my dad.

Very happy, my father embraced me affectionately, reminding me of the times he had held me as he told me his sorrows and the reason for his poverty. He worried that his children would continue to be enslaved by the forced labor that the governments ordered in those decades, keeping the Indigenous people in poverty.

"What did you ask that your children would do there on earth? What did you pray for them, according to the customs of your ancestors?"

My father responded, "I, I asked of Hunab' K'uh that my family and my children would be honored, that they would serve God, their people, and their community."

The leader of that chamber spoke again. "All that you have said has not yet come to pass. This son of yours has not fulfilled the promise you made and has not fully served his people and his land. Proof of that is that he is now here, because he is paying for his rejection of his land's cultural traditions. But since your son still has much life, it is not convenient that he stay here. He must return to earth and accept what has been asked for him. Only in this way can he fulfill what is written in the book of life for the destiny of each individual who is a guest on earth. But first, he must know part of the underworld so that on his return he will tell people everything he has seen here in the afterlife. May two guides accompany him on that dangerous journey, and may no one stop you. Of course, come back when it is prudent to return because this man has very limited time."

Then, to prepare me for the trip, he said, "Take this bundle that contains deer bones, a sprig of ocote and several ears of corn. We are sure they will serve you on your way to the place we are sending you."

I thanked the one who handed me the bundle, and I confirmed the objects mentioned were inside. When I saw that everything was there, I put it under my arms and checked that my huaraches were well tied, as I had to be ready for a difficult and dangerous journey. Then I took a straight stick as a cane, and so I was prepared to go to the place of eternal torture in the hands of the lords of evil.

The two assigned guides seemed very familiar to me, because they wore white clothing with the distinctive black *capixhay* as a coat. They also wore huaraches on their feet and woven palm leaf hats, like those I wore. Their presence gave me security, as I could tell just by looking at them, they were two courageous Maya ancestors who would watch over my safety. Unfortunately, I didn't recognize them, nor did they give me their name. Then, before leaving, and as a last warning, the man of the books told me:

"If, when you finally return, you wish to bring a clean body, you will need to take the path on the right. For now, it is necessary that you see some of the tortures and wicked tests in Xiwb'alb'a, so that upon your return you tell your countrymen what you have seen. To this place of suffering go those who disobey the natural law and the divine law, and those who do evil there on earth, those fooled by the evil angel who with his cunning and lies misleads them to this dark place that you will now know."

I had no courage to oppose these designs, and thus I bowed before the men as a sign of obedience and conformity. Meanwhile, my papa stroked my head again, insisting that I had patience and courage to resist the tests to which they would subject me. After he said goodbye to me, the assistants took him by the arms again to the place from which they had brought him.

I felt terribly sad to see my father disappear from my sight again after such a brief encounter. But I stood still, willing to accept everything that had been arranged for me in this place. At least now I realized it was possible to meet with loved ones who have preceded us on this trip of no return to the place of the dead, or *kamb'al.*

3

BEFORE THE DOOR TO XIWB'ALB'A

W E SET off, my two guides and I, down the road on the left. How attractive was that road, adorned by many flowers! Absorbed in my contemplation of that beauty, suddenly I saw approaching, with stealthy steps like hungry dogs, two pale men like the one who had tried to kidnap me earlier. Seeing my fear at the presence of those evil beings, my guides put me between them, giving me courage.

Those servants of the devil had approached us, and, throwing strange growls, they pointed at me like they wanted to snatch me from the hands of my guides. But these good spirits overcame the terrible threats of those hateful, bloodless beings. The one on my right told them, threatening:

"Listen, you devil's lackeys! If you believe that this man is one of yours, you are wrong; this man is still alive, and Divine Providence has allowed him, like few others, to step on this path of no return. It is necessary for him to realize the sufferings that Satan's followers undergo in order to tell of them when he returns to the earth. Begone from here, this man belongs not to you!"

Upon hearing these words of reprimand, they withdrew from us to return to the beginning of the path on the left, where they were supposed to receive and conduct the wretches who arrived with signs of mortal sin on their hands.

We continued walking along that beautiful and seductive path, which soon lost its beauty as we entered a gloomy enclosure. Even the flowers along the path appeared withered and entwined by thorns and filthy reptiles.

Timid as I was, I dared not ask anything about what my eyes at that moment witnessed. But one of my guides, as if guessing my thoughts, came forward to explain why that path had suddenly lost its splendor.

"What you see is identical to the path of short life on earth. In the earthly world, many people decide for easy life, and with great debauchery enjoy the pleasures of the world, destroying their lives and the lives of others. These people forget totally their soul, and many times knowing the truth, they see the way to deny it. Obviously, it is easier to satisfy the carnal desires than to feed the spirit. Here, then, is the stormy place to which vice and the abuse of life and nature on earth will lead. Those who travel these roads have chosen a fatal and painful end, eternally condemned to the darkness of Xiwb'alb'a where they will fulfill the punishment for their evil acts. But those who fight for life honestly, those who try to overcome difficulties with patience, those who have faith in Hunab' K'uh and who finally manage to win the battle of life against the deceptions of Matzualil, the devil, the path they take is the one on the right."

Here the paths of Xiwb'alb'a divided into four. The red path led to the place of the sun's emergence; the black, opposite the red, to where the sun went to hide; the white path toward the north; the yellow toward the south. Also, there was the vertical path leading upward and downward, blue-green, which is the one by which I came to this place, the path of life, since according to my guides I was still alive.

I could see clearly that the red path on the right was at first very steep and difficult to walk, but little by little it changed, until it culminated at the point where everything was perpetual joy and happiness, where the eternal light shines in the very heart of the universe. So I was thoughtful while I walked along with my guides, always inseparable.

They told me to follow the path towards the left, which is the path of the dead, until we arrived at the entrance of the cave that leads to the underworld. This is the door to Xiwb'alb'a, the place of unnamable fear. This damned, hateful door of pain and terror beyond limits was painted with chilling signs and phrases. There were also symbols of evil and nightmarish figures that made my teeth grind with fear and despair.

"*Okanh tata, okanh. Xchalo hawet hawu tinanh.*"

"*Oq'anh ninoj tawinh.*"

"Enter, man, enter. You have found what you sought."

"Enter and cry here for your misfortune."

"Leave all hope outside and receive what you deserve."

Many other phrases appeared, but I didn't read them because tears began to dull my sad eyes. Similar signs I saw engraved on that horrible door and on the black walls that seemed to crack from the hellish bustle they contained. In those moments I wanted to run away, to escape; but where, if the police and henchmen of Vukub' Q'aquix stalked me in every corner, showing me their evil, blood-smeared vampire fangs. I could not anyway, because at no point could I separate myself from my kind guides.

As my skin started to bristle with fear, I no longer wanted to go on, but we were forced to carry out that macabre journey, so I had to submit to my guides' words. Then, the huge door with hellish signs began to move slowly.

In that moment, as the great, evil door started opening, my legs buckled, and I collapsed in fear, unable to contain myself. I screamed, "No further! Please, let's go back!"

But my amiable guides knew my human weakness; they reassured me, saying, "Fear not, brother, we have been given the full power to go through this door that frightens and intimidates you. In the same way we enter this cursed place, so we will leave it, with no difficulties. Calm yourself, so that the lord of these gloomy mansions will not harm us, nor will anyone prevent us from continuing our journey, because we are protected. Arm yourself, then, with the courage necessary not to faint, because we will always be by your side to protect you from any danger."

Hearing these encouraging words, I clung to them to better shield myself in this fearful and dangerous place.

So we continued on our way, but the cursed atmosphere was already suffocating me. An intense and irresistible heat came from a terrifying enclosure where I, and no one, would ever wish to arrive.

"My Father! If, when I refer to this vision of the *kamb'al*, I still grieve and cry, give me encouragement to move forward with this story. I have to fulfill my mission, because those above commissioned me to make this known to those who would like to hear me here on the earth."

We advanced with great difficulty because we felt lost and without eyes in the eternal darkness. Suddenly my guides spoke with surprise, interrupting my meditations.

"Be careful! There is the guardian of Xiwb'alb'a!"

Hearing them, I looked with trepidation to see where they were pointing. Fear! The monstrous creature I beheld so terrified me that I nearly fainted. Concerned, my guides held me in their arms to give me courage and strength. Little by little I regained consciousness, as valor and strength returned to my trembling body. My heart almost stopped from the fear and dread that this infernal creature caused me. This was a monster or serpent with two heads that looked at us with burning eyes, ready to attack. I had heard of these types of gigantic snakes, called *xtx'anhal witz*, which are like the intestines of the mountains. These snakes sometimes come out from the underground bearing coffers of money on their backs, which the devil gives to those who ask for riches.

I was afraid this monstrous snake would strike at us, but that didn't happen. It became furious and uneasy about our presence, violently shaking its tail as if to whip us, but it remained quiet. Meanwhile, I walked on between my two guides, full of fear, looking from one side to another, afraid the henchmen of Vukub' Q'aquix would rip me from my guides' hands and tear me apart in their tremendous claws. I was afraid the three of us would fall into deadly traps set in our path by those same lords of Xiwb'alb'a.

My steps were not very secure because of the dense darkness that enveloped us. My guides, I saw, were also hesitating, not because they were afraid, but because they waited for me and saw with certainty the way they should lead me. The white glow emanating from them was the only light that illuminated our dreadful and dangerous path.

As I held fearfully to them, the three of us walked, slowly, advancing most cautiously to avoid falling into those deadly gorges. Oh, how dangerous this road was! For danger and death stalked us on all sides.

Thus my kind guides made their way through so much simmering danger, dodging everywhere the onslaught of the bloodless beings who would snatch me away. Despite the insistence of these evil ones to hinder our path, those who accompanied me, still more powerful, could make disappear the accursed traps and ensnarements that hindered our path.

The servants of Xiwb'alb'a were not happy with my presence, because I was not yet a resident of *kamb'al*, and this upset them. They wanted to make me fall into their evil traps, but my guides were already aware of their tricks, and they freed me from any trap they set for us.

We walked a bit through the darkness, and in the distance I began to see a strange forest, dark and noisy.

"Make ready the contents of your bundle!" ordered one of my guides. And the other said: "This is the realm of the *q'antz'ib' b'alam*, the jaguar."

I immediately reached into the bundle to do as they ordered. We cautiously approached a rocky path and could hear noises between the brambles behind the big rocks. Then, several hungry jaguars burst onto our path, and the enclosure rumbled with their shuddering roars. They were getting ready to pounce on us, so my guides ordered me to act without further delay.

"Take the deer bones from your bundle and throw them to the side of the road, where the hungry jaguars are stalking us."

Waiting not a second more, I pulled the deer bones from my backpack and threw them toward where the jaguars had gathered to attack us. When those bones fell near the hungry jaguars, they all pounced on the food. My guides took advantage of the moment of carelessness as the jaguars fought for the bones and ordered me to quickly cross that very dangerous enclosure.

But we could not go very far, as we entered an intensely dark tunnel, we could not see our way in the bowels of this cavern. Thousands of bats and vampires flew around me, as if they wanted to suck what little blood kept me alive. Those hellish bats screamed with hunger, desperate to pluck a piece of my nose or ears. I swatted the air uselessly, trying to scare away the accursed vampires who attacked me furiously, as if they hadn't tasted food for centuries.

"Light your ocotes!" my guides told me.

Quickly I took the bunch of ocote from my backpack and began to strike some stones to spark a fire. I put the ocotes together, and the fire came to light, illuminating the cavern and driving away the murderous bats.

"Well done, Antonio," my guides said, and I felt flattered by them.

Only then, with the ocote torches, could we cross that black tunnel to enter the place of true suffering. Here, already a faint clarity allowed me to see what was happening around me. So we continued our journey, always alert and seeing with a thousand eyes, though obscured, that path of many dangers and obstacles that slowed our march.

4

A DESERT IN FLAMES

W E HAD walked only a short distance when, like shocking thunder, loud cries of pain reached my ears. These lacerating screams, agonizing wails, complaints, insults, and other sinister howls came from those who found themselves immersed in that bustling hell. Terrified, I asked:

"What is it that forces these people to make such bone-chilling screams?"

My guides answered, "Come let us approach closer and you will perceive what happens there."

Slowly we approached that place from which emanated those desperate laments. It was a burning desert where gigantic flames burst out, enveloping all who were stuck there. The fire, as I saw, never consumed those who were in it, it only made them suffer horribly. I was shaken, hearing screams of terror and despair, infinite regrets that cursed everyone from the flames.

The relentless fire roared frightfully, lashing among its devouring flames the condemned who had no escape.

The unbearable heat from that accursed fire made me sweat in torrents, and just seeing them suffer, my soul filled with horror. How cruelly tormented were those poor lost souls!

As we stood overwhelmed, our eyes fixed on the scene we were witnessing, I vaguely heard bells tolling in the distance. Indeed, from far off I could hear slight sounds growing louder and louder. Then I could hear clearly the gloomy bells that ring for the dead and come from the earth.

Those distant remnants of echoes brought nostalgia to my ears. I was not mistaken. They were tolling chimes that reached these mansions as an announcement that one has departed from the living because of the death of the body and separation of the soul, which is the transition to this other life.

"Let us await here the arrival of the spirit whose human death the bells have announced on earth," said one of my guides.

Without responding to his indication, I stood still next to them, nearly immobilized.

There we stood, waiting at the edge of the pit of fire when she arrived at the secretariat of Xiwb'alb'a, the soul of this person who had left the land of mortals. Even though we were far away from the secretariat, we could see and hear what happened. It was an elderly lady and, because of the typical dress she wore, I was sure she came from my town. From afar we could see and hear what was happening as on a giant television screen. After having been examined and shown the good path to follow, she pleaded with the chief secretary to be taken to see where her comadre was, one who had preceded her on this trip without return. This lady insisted so much that they acceded to her pleas, allowing her to see the place her comadre occupied.

The recent arrival was taken to the precise place where we found ourselves now. Upon reaching the edge of that desert in flames, the lady asked her attendants:

"A year ago my comadre died. Where will she be? I want to thank her for a small favor she did to me on earth. She lent me money that I could not repay before she died."

Those who guided her answered, "Your comadre is here among those burning. This woman did more harm than good on earth. Shout her name and she will answer your call."

The lady paled when she saw the horrible flames that threatened to devour us too. Stepping back a little, the sad woman wiped the tears from her eyes, which looked more like two hot springs. Then, a bit calmed from the shock, she decided to call to her comadre. Her voice was almost inaudible over the rumbling noise produced by the flames, together with the complaints of the damned. Then, with more force she shouted again:

"*Kumaléééé . . . ! B'ay ayach kumaléééé!* Comadreeeee! Where are you, comadreeee?"

The lady's scream bounced between us like a voice magnified a thousand times. I had to cover my ears to keep from going deaf.

"*Kumaléééé . . . ! Kúúúúúúmaaaleeee!*"

"Comadre mía . . . ! Where are you? Comaaaaaadreeeee!"

A woman from the flames, upon hearing that scream mixed with the wails of pain, struggled to break through the entangled crowd, untying knots, separating bodies, heads, legs, and arms that squeezed her and prevented her from getting out.

It took a long time for the woman in the flames to free herself from her companions and finally emerge to the surface. With a shove she came forward and revealed her gaunt and sad appearance. She was not the same as before. She had changed radically, totally disfigured. She looked like an ember that burned without producing flames. Thus, like the ray that flashes its broken gold form in the sky, and then instantly disappears between the black clouds that originated it, this was the time that the meeting of the two comadres lasted. The punished woman managed to get her head out of the flames for a brief moment, then submerged again without even giving her time to say a word.

Seeing this site of bloody agony and the sad situation of her comadre, the one who had called burst into tears, sobbing and retorting in this way.

"Oh my friend, you did me a favor, and so I came to thank you, but I never thought you would go to such a horrible place. Huuuuuu . . . !"

So crying, she was removed from that chamber and immediately taken to the right place, where she belonged.

As they carried this woman out of that darkness, I wanted to run and join her, so overwhelming was my terror. All I knew was that each movement took us deeper into the depths of Xiwb'alb'a.

Seeing my reaction and understanding my weaknesses, my guides held me back, saying, "Do not go! We must remain longer here in this place of intense pain. However, we should divert to another tunnel and not continue to descend into the depths, because you are weak and will not be able to bear the visions in Xiwb'alb'a's lowest levels."

I felt better, thinking soon we would leave this damned place, and so I was calm with them. Why would I oppose my guides, if they kindly took care of me and led me in that dark place? Where would I want to go without them? I stood blushing over what I had just done.

They looked upon me again with benevolent eyes and gently reassured me: "Calm down, nothing will happen while we are with you."

So I stayed next to my guides, but I did not understand anything that happened there. Nor could I articulate any word, so horrified as I was. Then one of my guides spoke like this: "This is the place where the evil murderers of minors go."

I turned my eyes back to that place, and again the tears began to moisten my irritated eyes. And my guide kept talking. "The lady who just showed herself from the flames was a murderer and kidnapper in life. Look carefully at the position these soulless people occupy here in Xiwb'alb'a."

This was just what he told me; and for my part I can say that today the consciousness of human dignity has been lost. Therefore, it is necessary to avoid these extremes and educate sons and daughters in respect for life. Without respect, love, and compassion, we become instruments of death. Deserving of her punishment was that lady!

So much thinking detained my steps, so my guides urged me on, saying, "We must keep to our march and not let ourselves be detained because we have been given a small time to complete this tour."

The other said: "Before we leave this level of Xiwb'alb'a, we shall see what there is in that other cavern, close to the desert in flames."

I began to walk more quickly next to them to go see this other place of eternal suffering; here is where one knows the true meaning of the word pain.

Thus we arrived at the edge of a pit of boiling blood. From this unusual place came the insults and terrified screams of those submerged. I asked my guides: "Who are these unfortunates who suffer without measure here among the boiling blood in Xiwb'alb'a?"

One of them answered immediately: "In this place are the wicked, those great oppressors, criminals, and genocides who caused so much innocent blood to be spilled over the earth."

Oh what horror! While my guides and I were contemplating that enclosure, we saw coming from the distance a man torn to shreds, running and running madly. He was wearing armor and carrying a sword in his hand, but he could not defend himself because behind him came hundreds of Xiwb'alb'a guards and officers, also armed with slings, spears, bows and arrows, who chased him and beat him without ceasing. The man ran and fell in terror, screaming desperately like a wounded dog with no one to defend him.

What caused his crazy and demonic flight? Where did that wretch think he could find refuge in this place of tortures? Everything was dark, and the pitiful man fell like one demented or terribly drunk.

This was like a simulation of a battle the man had lost. When cornered on the banks of the pit of boiling blood, the same wretch threw himself headlong into the pit to defend himself among his companions. All the guards and officers chasing him gathered to witness the scene of pain, rejoicing in their triumph.

Unable to move before that nameless horror, I saw how the demon guards and officers departed happily, accustomed as they were to playing with this personage in the pit of boiling blood. This blood, according to my guides, was the blood of all the victims of wars, massacres, and genocide.

Meanwhile, the one who had thrown himself into the boiling blood began to be torn apart and strangled by his same companions in tragedy, who, finding nowhere to express their anger, mutilated each other. Seeing that everyone was annihilating him, I dared to ask: "Who is that person who came and seems to be despised by the devil himself?"

"This wretch, whose spirit you see here mutilated, is the bloody conqueror Pedro de Alvarado. You will no longer remember what happened to your ancestors some four hundred years ago, but this is the one that hanged and burned Indigenous rulers in their towns and nations. Many of them, the conquerors are here, irrational men who killed and enslaved entire peoples they called 'Indians.' This scene of their persecution is reenacted here in Hell as an eternal drama of immense pain, as well as that caused to others," they replied.

The presence of that evil being so close to me felt disturbing. Tonatiuh Avilantaro was the one who destroyed entire cities and burned without mercy rulers and leaders. This was the conqueror who made thousands suffer and endure what was called the war of conquest. His cruelty was that of a man possessed, and he caused intense pain and misery to the people he slaughtered; this was now the cause of his bloody ordeal. Here, then, were the most violent and hateful conquerors and genocides of all time. Among them, Tonatiuh or Pedro de Alvarado, who is now one of the main inhabitants of Xiwb'alb'a.

It was sad to see this moving scene and at the same time very terrible; it made me sweat blood and grind my teeth in fear and despair. At least I could say upon my return to earthly life that the great genocides of all time were not loved even by Vukub' Q'aquix himself, "Seven Fires," Lucifer.

"Let us depart!" I shouted. "I can't stand to see all these people in eternal agony."

Seeing my mood, my kind guides took me by the hand again and led me quickly to another place. This time, we diverted from the path that went down into the depths, and so now I felt more strength to continue the journey.

Oh, how terrible are the tortures and tests here in Xiwb'alb'a, the mansion of the Lords of Evil! Nothing then, of the bad or good that is done, however little, will be forgotten by the Creator. All will be written in the book of life; and this perfect chronicle of all our acts, filed in the divine library, will be the infallible testimony when we are judged by the Supreme Judge in the consummation of the centuries. This is what the priests and missionaries have repeated to our people since they arrived among us.

"Continue, continue walking," my guides insisted; and so I kept walking alongside them, full of thoughts.

5

THE SPRINGBOARD OF DEATH

SHORTLY AFTER we resumed our walk, we came upon another fierce servant of Xiwb'alb'a hysterically driving along two people with whips and flagellation. They were a woman and man who wailed as they walked, with the executioner instructing them brutally. This demonic guard inflicted tremendous lashings, leaving their bodies thoroughly bruised and discolored. I have never seen someone so harsh and heartless as this raging demon thrashing these defenseless bodies.

"Walk, you accursed ones! Walk, you wretches! Don't stop, you pieces of shit!"

With such great vulgarity spoke this accursed muleteer, while never ceasing to whip his victims. He pounded them as mercilessly as if those two sufferers were beasts of burden refusing to walk.

As the poor unhappy people moved along with fatigue and pain, the executioner at one point violently stopped them where the road was divided into two. The road to the right had white boards atop the silt, like a type of carpet. Those who traveled this strange road had to walk on the boards to avoid getting dirty with the mud.

This path, I could see, was very little used because it did not belong to the paths of Xiwb'alb'a. It was a path that led upward, toward another level, so at this point the damned always had to stop to see for the last time the happiness of the Father's blessed ones. As I could tell, Xiwb'alb'a had passages or portals that connected with the world above so that those who suffered could see the happiness they had lost.

Returning my eyes to the path of the white boards, with great surprise I saw that in the distance a married couple, Maltixh Not and Moncha Koy, came with determined and triumphant steps. They wore bright new clothes in the style of the Jakaltek Maya. The lady was wearing a beautiful colored ribbon that curled her black hair, tied to her head like a crown. Her cut of green wool rolled to her waist combined beautifully with the white huipil that radiated and illuminated them both. The gentleman was also dressed in the old-fashioned Jakaltek style: white blanket pants and shirt, leather huaraches and a short-brimmed hat. On his waist he wore a blue sash, and he smiled very happily. The dress of the two, in fully typical Jakaltek attire, along with their language; everything identified me with them. This elderly Jakaltek couple had been very rich, but despite their wealth they lived with humility and helped many poor people in the town. When there were famines, they distributed their corn to those who needed it, and even when they sold it, they did so at a very low price to help the poor and needy.

Upon seeing me near them, the two became very happy and said to me, "*Kaw chonhtzalah hach jilnian. Niman chawute ha k'ul tata, ch'elotoj hune' ilweb'ail ti' tawu* . . . We are very glad to see you here. Have patience, Tata, because you will pass this test. Keep struggling and working because the end is beautiful. Don't let yourself be fooled by wicked tongues. Don't join the gossipers, because they are the ones who will screw you over. And if, when you definitely return to this place, you come as clean as now, you will occupy the empty room next to ours. There, look and see, in that garden."

Thus they spoke, simply, like the ancient people of the town.

At the end of that path of the white boards they lived in the middle of a beautiful garden that surrounded their scented rooms. In truth, I would like to live in such a beautiful place. Brief then was our meeting, and I thanked them for their good advice. When they finished talking and saying goodbye, they returned along the same path of the white boards from whence they came.

After this sudden encounter with people I knew well, my guides and I closely followed that guard who led his prisoners fiercely down the narrow path on the left. Again they stopped, this time at the entrance to a filthy morass. Here lay two long, narrow marking sticks that came together at the foot of a ladder which emerged from between two thick posts. These two posts were also joined at the top by a thick, strong loop. The structure looked like a springboard or a gallows to hang those sentenced to death.

Then, the demon who led them ordered the man to go ahead, and he did so. The two had no alternative, as they had reached the place where they had to serve their sentence. But . . . why did they deserve this tragic place?

My guides, as if guessing my thoughts, explained to me: "These two people are the prototype of liars, slanderers, and traitors. They are the ones who delivered their villages to the invaders and denounced their community, facilitating the invasion and genocide of their own people. They are those who denounced their neighbors during the wars, betraying their people and their villages. Because of them, thousands of people lost their lives during the wars of conquest and colonization."

Meanwhile, I kept looking to see how those wretched ones would take their punishment. With great difficulties, the man traversed the two marking sticks, trying to maintain balance so as not to sink into the rot. He walked slowly, swinging on the boards until he reached the bottom of the ladder in the middle of the two posts. There he wanted to stop, seeing the abyss on whose shore he had arrived, but the executioner ordered him to mount the strange springboard.

When the man stood on the platform above the ladder, the evil guard approached him jubilantly, skipping and jumping as if in some merry *danse macabre*. After this frenetic dance, the devil's lackey kicked at one of the posts like a burro. As a result, the unhappy man was propelled outward, turning great and horrible somersaults in the air, as do expert swimmers or divers. But that sad sinner did not fall into water; I could not see in the distance where he had fallen, I could only tell that he was stung somewhere in that black abyss, releasing a horrible cry of fear and desperation: "Aaaaaaaaayyyyyyyy!"

His anguished scream shook my body violently, and I felt much compassion for that condemned man.

Seeing what happened to her partner, the woman wanted to flee back down the path of the white boards, but her guardian seized her by the hair. The woman did not want to cross that swamp and reach the springboard of death, but the ruthless guard wanted to complete his task; he struck her harder, forcing her to walk. Upon reaching the foot of the posts, the woman stopped again, screaming in despair. "No, I don't want to go up, have pity!"

But her executioner, deaf to her screams and unmoved by her pleas, gave her more lashes until the woman had to climb the steps to take her punishment. The woman cried inconsolably and begged for mercy, but that just made the devil become angrier. When the woman stood on the platform above, the fearsome executioner approached again, leaping with joy, until that bulgy-eyed enforcer howled like a ferocious wolf, directing a kick at the second post.

Just as it had happened with the man, the woman shot off with horrible pirouettes into the air, until she and her ghastly screams disappeared at the bottom of that abyss. Oh, cruelty of the devil! He mercilessly fulfilled the fate of his followers.

I stood there terrified! So many people fell into those infernal lodgings, and it horrified me to see them suffer. Thousands upon thousands, countless were the unfortunates of different peoples, nations, creeds, and religions. All who committed these crimes fell into the abyss like dried leaves taken up by the wind.

"Now, you go up!" my guides told me.

"No, I don't want to go up! I'm scared! Please, no!" I told them in horror, almost fainting.

"Don't be afraid to climb, because nobody will hit the posts to make you fall!" they answered me with a compassionate tone:

Confiding in their words, I began to walk on those dirty sticks, which at the moment I felt sinking under my weight. Several times I wanted to go back, afraid that the treacherous guard would follow me; but I was reassured to see he remained motionless beside my guides.

Little by little I ascended the ladder, but always afraid someone would come touch one of the posts. As I laid my crippled feet on the platform above, suddenly the hateful executioner wanted to rush to the posts and hurl me, unsuspecting, to the abyss. But my guides, attentive to all his movements, kept him back, knocking him down into the mud. My guides, my dearest protectors, could never leave me. That was why the evil servant of Xiwb'alb'a failed in his attempt because I was not helpless. I had my bodyguards, secure and invincible, protecting me at every moment.

The soulless lackey remained there a long time, struggling to get out of that filth. Meanwhile, with extreme care, I grabbed the loop at the top and looked with wonder down below, but I couldn't see anything. The huge pit seemed to have no bottom, because everything looked black, eternally black. The eye could not penetrate into that blackest abyss.

From the platform I could catch the distant screams coming from the dark depths. It seemed amid some swirling wind the souls were blowing and colliding with others sunk in the blackness of that abyss.

An asphyxiating wind emerged from the murmuring precipice and almost overcame me. For that reason I rushed back down the stairs, afraid the hurricane would drag me down below. Pale with fright I went to meet with my guides who awaited me, anxious and very attentive.

Back beside my protectors, my fear diminished. Then, less agitated and without knowing how, my lips produced this question whose answer was obvious: "Can these damned escape this abyss?"

To which my kind guides responded promptly: "Never! No one will ever be able to reach the other shore, because when a soul has arrived at this site it is impossible to leave it."

This is what they told me, while they encouraged me to continue our frightful journey. With my insecure steps we resumed our march, because the time they had given us to remain in this place of torture was limited.

We had not yet reached the exit of that chamber when I heard the sound of a loud hammering from a cave on the edges of the path on which we walked.

"Let us go see what is happening there," said my guides.

And I, like a meek little lamb, followed them without opposing their decisions. As we entered that room, a great panic seized me when I saw a multitude of men working without rest, breaking large solid rocks. These condemned souls had in their hands some very heavy mallets or hammers with which they wearily beat the unbreakable granite boulders. It seemed like a Xiwb'alb'a mine, from which the lord of the mountain could obtain minerals to offer for the purchase of souls from those who made deals with the devil. Many, to obtain quick money, make pacts with the lord of the mountain, and now have to pay with punishments for this corruptly-made money. In this place also were the encomenderos who had forced the poor to work in their mines. So just as they enslaved people to break stones for them, so they too were suffering what in life they made others suffer.

Poor men, never will they finish this cursed labor of sweat and moans, pain and weariness. Like a dirty little stream, hot and bitter drops ran down the filthy bodies of these sad condemned men. Rivers of sweat ran under their feet, rotting their toes. Interminable was the toil of these wretched workers here in Xiwb'alb'a. Oh, terrible despair, to find oneself cruelly tormented by this endless and exhausting work!

Some furiously threw hammer blows at the rocks as if they wanted to finish their task quickly. Others, in their heated fatigue, collapsed completely from unbearable exhaustion. Thirst burned their lips, and their mouths radiated like a furnace — for when they spat, they spat fireballs. No one deigned to approach them with a glass of cold water. Goodness was dead among these wicked ones who were mistreated by their hateful Xiwb'alb'a foremen.

I did not ask my guides why these wretches were suffering, as I already understood, but I did open my mouth to ask for water. The heat of this place made me very thirsty, so I asked my guides to take me to a source to quench the unrelenting thirst that consumed me.

"I am very thirsty!" I cried to them, as if my lips were aflame.

"What are you telling us? You must know that throughout this trip you will not be able to drink or receive anything that is offered here. If you receive food or drink from those who live in this other life, you will no longer be able to return to your village. Come on, let us hurry to get you out of this accursed place soon," my guides explained compassionately.

Saying no more, I raised my head reverently before them as a sign of obedience to their words. And so we continued our macabre tour of the bowels of Xiwb'alb'a, the place of death.

6

FOREVER DRUNK

DISTRACTED AND confused from what I had seen and heard, I barely
noticed the distance from one place to the next. So we arrived
at another dark compound here in Xiwb'alb'a, the dwelling
place of the lords of evil. Upon entering we stopped abruptly, for
on the noxious ground, with faces mired in their own vomit, lay
many, many drunks.

The place was full of noise. In one corner some mariachis were
singing corridos about the devil and his immoral adventures, while
the depraved souls poisoned the environment with the smoke of
their cigars and other cursed potions they were consuming. It was
all here, like some replica of what happens there on earth.

To the beat of this raucous music, some drunks tried to dance,
but what they did was no dancing—more like shaking their bodies
with strange, forceful convulsions, like puppets with no control.
They beat each other violently like crazed, furious madmen. All
were unrecognizable, as their faces and bodies were swollen from
so much abuse. They fell and got back up, brutalized by the liquor
they consumed without ceasing.

It was horrible to see them in their agony, their hangovers tor-
menting them with irresistible headaches. Everyone who passed

by on that path trampled on their faces and spat on their mouths. They looked, then, like earthworms in pig's slop, or the pigs themselves, wallowing in their rot.

In that same place some marimbistas were playing the song of death. The frantic atmosphere rumbled with the shrill, monotonous noises from their marimbas. Here was an eternal and accursed disorder, the essence of chaos, with all sorts of perversities, led by Matzualil himself at a macabre feast. Some clutched at each other and others slashed their machetes furiously, maddened by the alcohol. Still others sucked, cried, screamed, and rolled around, completely drunk.

The wasted ones insulted and fought each other, drawing blood as if they were madmen or vampires hungry for revenge. Nothing satisfied their tastes and their infernal follies. The cursed alcohol went to their heads, numbing their senses until they acted like true wild beasts.

The marimbistas were drunk too. Their fingers were excessively swollen and blistered, and it caused them great difficulty to raise their arms under the heavy mallets and keep playing. The old marimba they played no longer produced the sweet, dreamy melodies it should have. Instead, gushing forth from its keyboard were groans of pain and eternal despair. In this way, the old marimba was torn to pieces in crazy music by those rough, dirty hands, drumming in complete disorder.

As if that weren't enough, in another corner adorned with bottles of güaro, there was also the barmaid, who worked to distribute her poisonous concoction to all those present.

In any street feast at any place, she was a principal element of the festivities. So there she was, presiding over that monstrous scene and dispatching *cusha* and *chicha* and shots of *pox* to the drunks who danced uncontrollably.

This filthy woman had a red cloth tied so tightly on her head that her eyes, like flames of fire, seemed to bulge out. She screamed out shrilly, incessantly offering liquor to the dancing drunks. Sometimes she would push some of them out of her premises because she no longer wanted to see them vomit on the muddy ground.

Everyone in this chamber suffered from terrible headaches that drove them mad. They grabbed hold of their hair and threw themselves to the ground, desperately seeking to flee their excruciating pain. They beat themselves terribly, spilling their blood in torrents that ran like boiling water over their bodies and fed the filthy worms that swarmed in the puddles of sunken drunks.

The pestilential odor of that place made them empty their stomachs continuously; right there in full view they would shit and urinate. In vain they tried to refuse the damned bottles of güaro the bartender offered them. What's more, from those dirty bottles ironic laughter seemed to emanate, groans and creepy howls that further horrified those unhappy people.

Here, then, is the bitter consequence of the cursed drink that leads to perdition and damages humanity. Many homes are destroyed, many children die or live in extreme misery because of unconscious parents dominated by the vice of alcohol. Some become thieves, others murder under the effect of this cursed concoction that is the urine of Vukub' Q'aquix.

As these crude thoughts wandered through my mind, I couldn't tell if we were still walking or not. My guides brought me back to reality, saying: "Wake up, in front of and behind those mounds is something you must watch carefully."

We emerged from out of a narrow passage into what seemed a completely dry and desolate field. Soon I noticed what my guides had told me about, two mounds covered in sand, burning in the heat. When we got close enough, my guides told me again: "Now, go up to see what is behind those small hills."

With no time to tell them yes or no, I suddenly found myself halfway down the road. The path was very steep and dangerous, and some stones slipped down from the weight of my body. With many efforts and difficulties, I managed to get to the top where the tips of these two hills or twin mounds separated.

Before a moment passed I discovered behind these burned hills many chained men, their eyes sparkling as if they were two burning balls of fat. Their tongues burned too, and they spit loud flames from their mouths. They truly looked like human torches.

Oh what horror! Those men writhed and squirmed, wanting to break their chains, but they will never succeed.

Among them was J.R., who on seeing me wanted even more to get out of his bonds, but vain was his effort. He could not move from his designated place in the ferment. I recognized him immediately because this wicked man had died a couple of years ago.

Who didn't know J.R.? He was the owner of the store on the edge of town where they were always committing crimes. He was a recruiter among the owners of the large fincas to bring crews of workers to the coasts. He got them into debt, so they had to go down to the coast to work in inhospitable places, returning with dysentery and malaria. And for those who did manage to make some money, J.R. took it off them because he was a usurer as well as being a heavy drunk. Every day he stayed drunk and stole to keep his damn vice. He abused his body a lot, dragging it through the mud and never wanting to listen to those who tried to help him separate himself from his vice. He himself asked to condemn himself, because when they avoided him, he responded mockingly. "Saint güaro, your kingdom come. Pour me another one as I pawn my charro."

And so he kept drinking, not just for a day but weeks and weeks. No one could stop his hand because he loved the güaro, and when he was more loaded, he kept asking with grunts: "Bartender, serve me more, because I want to drink with my buddy Satan."

He drank so much it seemed his bottle of *cusha* was stuck to his face. He barely slept, because then he would wake up, covered in shit and urine, and continue with the same fury as always. One such day, tired of the life he led, he hung himself on a tree on the edge of town.

Here is the place where he had arrived along with the dictators and oppressors whom he served as foreman, stripping the campesinos and enslaving them with forced labor. He wanted to speak, but since the fire burned his mouth and tongue, he could only produce a few chilling wheezes. He was muttering, but his words seemed to come out of his burning mouth as flames.

There I left him, and I fled from that place of the enchained. He wanted to follow me, but his strong bonds prevented it. He was crying, never to escape his eternal captivity.

I rushed down from the summit, covered in sweat, to where my guides eagerly awaited me. When I reached them, they held me in their hands, wiping the sweat away. I stopped for a moment to rest until my fatigue abated and we continued on our way.

"Now you see!" My guides told me. "Here in the depths of Xiwb'alb'a are the drunkards and those who created this cursed vice for them. Poverty makes them suffer, and they look for alcohol as their refuge; therefore, those who have humiliated and exploited them for centuries are also here paying for the destruction of so many lives."

I remembered at once the suffering of the people in my town. Poverty is not natural for us Indigenous people, but an imposition that began a *b'aktun* ago—four hundred years. People lived happily before the arrival of the *uwes* who came from across the sea. Then began the suffering of our people, looking for a way out of that colonial hell. The alcohol has been a concoction for escape, but it was not always so. Alcohol used to be a ceremonial element that did not create vice among our people. Now, it is the sadness, oppression, and despair of many Indigenous people that leads them to get drunk to feel better and forget their sorrows for a moment. According to my ancestors, the joy or suffering experienced on earth is repeated in the afterlife.

Again, I started thinking about the drunks who don't want to rectify themselves and resume family responsibilities. If everyone thought of God, the world would not be as cruel as it is today, but our minds are very closed, and we don't want to know anything about the beyond. The existence of the soul, like all divine mysteries, is very much about man's reason and not against reason. We need great faith to believe in what our blind eyes don't see. These things and more I was thinking, so that once again I did not realize how we had entered another dark and bustling room of Xiwb'alb'a.

7

FEATHERS ON A HEN

W E PROGRESSED slowly, as difficulties mounted in our path. I frequently stumbled over obstacles that hindered our steps, but my guides, always attentive to any danger, protected me with their blessed hands.

"Come here, look at those suffering women," they said to me now, pointing at another dismal place.

I turned my eyes immediately to the spot he indicated. Hundreds of women were there, weeping together for their misfortune. Each woman had a chicken in her hands, in open view to those walking on that road. We could see they were very tired, as they stretched and shrank like worms among ants, inconsolably moaning. Seeing them in such a moving situation afflicted my heart, and tears of sad compassion began flowing from my weary eyes.

I went up very close to one of them to try to recognize her, but I couldn't. Instead she, perhaps seeing the tears welling up in my eyes, said to me almost screaming, "If you feel so sorry for us seeing us suffer, put something soft under my knees to rest my wounds and calm my pain a little. Quick cabrón, I can't take it anymore!"

Thus she spoke in a commanding tone, and I, out of compassion, wanted to put anything I could under her mutilated knees to appease her pain. It really broke my heart to see this woman suffer, kneeling there in view of all those who passed by that path. Then one of my guides, hearing what she said to me and seeing my charitable attitude, stopped me, while the other addressed the wretch.

"Condemned woman! How dare you be so haughty as to order that your punishment be diminished? Be quiet and carry out your punishment, as this is what you asked for. Nobody can ever alleviate your pain. Ah, brazen woman, who does not lose her pride!" My guide spoke to her so severely that she felt humiliated and bit her lips, then without lifting her eyes continued her endless work of counting the feathers on a black hen.

Seeing how the woman was counting feathers of this repugnant bird, I asked her: "Listen, unfortunate woman! What is your punishment, that you must count this black hen's feathers?"

She raised her head heavily and replied: "I, oh living soul! I was a resident of your same town. But you see that you no longer recognize me due to this cruel state in which I find myself. My name is R . . . , and I was a chicken thief. Wretched me, for I am guilty of my own situation."

Saying this, she lowered her head sheepishly as if desperately remembering the dire course of her life back on the earthly world. Then she continued.

"Yes, I was a thief, a vile thief! I stole chickens from my neighbors and blamed other people. I would laugh when they told me there was a hell. I thought it was just a made-up word to scare people, but the truth is not so; I came here to see and feel it. Look how I am now, sunk down in this hell, where the demons don't stop coming to beat you. Alas, disgraced are we to be here condemned! This is what we get for being stupid donkeys. Ay, chingado, jodido, mierda!"

She kept struggling to talk through her copious crying, and her words would get stuck in her throat. Then, she continued, "Since

I left the earthly world, sadly I came to fall into this accursed place where I find myself now. Every day I'm here on my knees on the hard ground, counting the feathers on this damned chicken. This hen is the product of my constant thieving, and here I am exhibited before the eyes of all those who mock me. As you can see, here I count and recount this chicken's feathers, without rest, for when I get close to the last feather, the damn bird shakes itself and makes me lose count. My efforts have been useless, because here I have been counting and counting without being able to finish. I am convinced that I will never finish this damned job that torments me. So here I have been stuck, ridiculed by those who pass by, spitting at me without compassion and shouting at me, 'chicken thief.' My punishment is to be huddled here, counting and counting a thousand and thousand times the feathers of this filthy hen, enduring it every time the damned thing shakes, then losing count and being confused forever. I feel very sore and completely miserable, because this damned hen never calms down and won't let me count her feathers."

The lady slapped the head of the chicken that would not stop shaking its wings to confuse the count. Then, she looked at me with sad eyes and continued telling me her sorrows: "In addition to dealing with this chicken, I also have to put up with these demons that keep beating their victims. But never mind, I wanted this, that's why I stole shamelessly. Now it's led me to the gran chingada! I wanted this like a fool, a donkey, an idiot. Who would be shaking me like this if I had been good to my neighbors? Ah, if only I hadn't messed around so much! What good did it do me? Am I eating from my robberies now? On the contrary, this damned chicken has been pecking at me so hard that it almost gouges out my eyes."

In that precise moment the black hen shook her feathers violently, confusing the woman in her count. Then, very irritated, she began to wring the neck of the horrible chicken, who, in response, pecked and scratched terribly at the condemned woman's face.

The woman began to count again, starting with the tail: "One, two, three, four, five, six, seven, eight, nine, ten . . . , fifteen . . . , thirty . . . , fifty . . . , one-hundred fifty. . . ."

The chicken then shook again with more force, and in the same way the woman again had to start over: "One, two, three, four, five, six, seven, eight, nine, ten . . . , fifteen . . . , thirty . . . , fifty . . . , one-hundred fifty. . . ."

When the count was close to finishing, the filthy chicken shook itself again. So the feather count went on forever and ever. The woman turned to see me and in a plaintive voice expressed these words of advice: "When you go back there to earth, tell people everything you see here. People need to know of the punishments that await thieves here in this other life. And if some are doing it, they can ask for forgiveness and not do it again so that they don't come among us, because as you see, everyone who does evil comes here to receive their punishment."

Only this could she tell me, because the hysterical demons in charge down there began to scream furiously and thrash their whips, to make all those souls work faster counting the feathers of those incessantly pecking chickens. I turned away from the woman and followed my guides, walking among all the condemned, both men and women in the same situation. Some were crying; others, with wide eyes, saw us pass. What desolation we saw in this enclosure!

We couldn't advance far because some chicken eggs blocked our path. They rolled and rolled like round stones in our way, trying to trip us. Near us was another large group of the condemned, suffering from these strange eggs. When they tried to go forward, the eggs rolled under their feet, and thus they fell crashing to the ground. Those mysterious eggs did not stop, always in constant motion, knocking down those beings who tried to walk or flee this enclosure.

Then, one of my guides told me in a very laconic way: "These convicts are related to the previous ones. These are also chicken and egg thieves."

I could not fully comprehend the meaning of what my guide wanted to explain, but I could see many kinds of trials and torture here in Xiwb'alb'a, as everything that is done bad or good on earth has its punishment or its reward.

Those wretches couldn't stand up for a moment before they would fall and crash their noses on the rocky ground. Those who remained lying on the ground for a long time were beaten with clubs by the sadistic guards who enjoyed torturing them. It was a game, but a hellish game that made the damned cry.

Those eggs were unbreakable. I confirmed it with one that came rolling at my feet, knocking me down. Annoyed, I got up and kicked the egg, which bounced off the nose of one of the watching guards. When he felt the blow, he was enraged and wanted to snatch me from the hands of my two protectors. But my guides came out in front, restraining the fury of that menacing imp. Startled, I cowered like a puppy between my two guides, avoiding the Vukub' Q'aquix foreman's touch.

Seeing that this demon was still foolish enough to try to capture me, my guides seized him by the hands and feet, and between the two of them they cast him like a dead dog among the rolling eggs. When the demon crashed to the ground, his companions, far from getting angry, laughed to see how my guides were playing with him. They cackled out loud, while the other struggled to stand up. The joke did not last long, because when he managed to stand up, he quickly joined his companions. Then he pointed at me angrily and whispered to the others something I could not understand.

My guides, guessing what those evil ones were planning, quickly took my hand and led me through the rolling eggs. In my guides' presence the strange eggs were pushed aside, letting us escape easily. Then, when those demon guards wanted to follow us, the eggs began rolling so fast they made our pursuers slip and fall. Thus we escaped from the hands of those unfortunates, as they uttered insults instead of reaching us.

But we could not go very far, because the road led us to another room where we were met by crazy giant hens who wanted to attack us. A peck from one of these huge chickens could've torn out my eyes or ears. To keep me from being attacked, my guides ordered me: "Get your corn ready because you're going to need it here!"

Hearing this, I reached into my bundle, pulled out the ears of white and yellow corn, and tossed them to the side of the road toward the monstrous chickens. Seeing the corn, the hungry chickens pounced on those ears, pecking at them to pluck the kernels. While the chickens were busy eating the grains of corn, my guides and I quickly crossed the room.

My nerves calmer from having passed those tests, I thought again of the women counting feathers and the rolling eggs. I reminded myself then that among the Mayas stealing eggs or chickens was a very serious sin, perhaps because the egg or chicken thief thus deprives a poor family of their livelihood. I don't know, but I didn't dare ask my guides why stealing eggs has a very special punishment. Nor did they explain it to me, so I was left with that doubt.

"Let us make haste!" they told me, and I, without responding, followed their steps so as not to fall behind.

8

DECEIVED YOUNG WOMEN

MY TOES were bleeding from all my stumbles as I had fled to escape those angry demons, but I kept walking. Once we were far from that place, I sat down to calm my fast breathing and pacify my disturbed nerves. My guides seemed calmer than I was, as they kept chatting and looking at me with a certain compassion, as if to say: "Poor man, let us see if he can handle the path."

Fortunately, we had gotten far away from those violent demons and beyond the reach of the hoarse voices of the women who cursed their luck, their lives, and their misfortune here in Xiwb'alb'a. I was most grateful to my guides who prepared me for this trip with those ears of white and yellow corn that saved us from the horrible, bewitched chickens.

"We shall rest for a moment, and then we'll find a short way to get to the exit. We see you are exhausted, and for this reason we must return as soon as possible," they said.

I rested briefly and then my guides encouraged me to keep going. And so I followed them, still sweating, because I didn't want to lag behind. That macabre walk had to end, because I already felt like

I was dying. The good thing was that my guides were with me and patted me on the back to cheer me up and strengthen my spirit.

We again changed our course by taking a portal upward, so that we emerged from the depths, but always penetrating into the unknown. Suddenly, joyous laughter made us stop.

In a beautiful spring, many young women were laughing while bathing naked. Their long, beautiful hair slid down their backs and they laughed without a care. Those who were on the shore waiting to enter the water wore transparent and seductive suits. They giggled as if they were truly happy. Some were swimming calmly, while others talked and laughed as they happily washed clothes on the banks of the spring. Those women were beautiful. With little clothing on, half-naked they went up to hang the clothes they washed on the green bushes on the banks of the spring. I was very surprised to see this joy where there was supposed to be pain and suffering. All of that was inexplicable to me. Although yes, we had climbed to a higher level or circle of Xiwb'alb'a, instead of going down.

"Let us move closer," ordered my guides, and slowly we approached the spring.

We had not yet reached the women when their outbursts of laughter turned at once into terrifying screams, cries, and sobs. It was such a sudden change that it puzzled me. That happy scene had become a place of wailing and tremendous pain.

Seeing this abrupt change from joy to sadness and pain, I asked my guides, "What is wrong with these women, and why do they now scream instead of laugh? Who are they?"

They responded: "These women remain here bathing eternally; but the current running under this white foam and reaching their waist, rises to high temperatures, causing this fomentation. This is how the water in this pool starts to boil, burning them to the navel, and thus they are stuck forever. Then the water cools down, little by little, until they feel good again and laugh again. So, in turn, they cry and laugh for eternity in this underground spring."

"And if you want to know who they are," continued the other, "we will tell you that they were abused and became prostitutes. They never married and neither did they insist on undoing marriages, nor did they engage in these immoral acts of their own free will. These poor women were deceived and even forced to dedicate themselves to selling their bodies. Those who had power and control of the towns abused them, enslaving and prostituting them. Other times, extreme poverty pushed them into this vice of prostitution when they could find no other means to subsist. Some were abandoned by their parents, leaving them exposed to all these social problems. They themselves do not bear all the blame for their actions, because they did not act according to their will. First they were forced, and they got used to that way of life."

As my guide was explaining this situation, suddenly the women stopped their screaming and returned to their normal state, to laugh again.

"These women have moments of joy and pain. They are condemned here, never being able to separate themselves from this spring where they alternately suffer and delight."

My guide continued speaking, while he pointed his finger to the other side of the strange spring, where from a great furnace terrifying screams rang out. Inside this hot oven were men and women screaming and asking to be freed from this torture. Then one of my guides spoke.

"Here are those who deceived the young women at the spring. These are the lords and ladies with power who enslaved the young women not only as servants but as concubines. This mistreatment toward the people whose villages they invaded was so painful that Hunab K'uh himself wept in his heart when he saw them suffer for centuries. Here they are, these criminals who kidnapped, abused, and even killed their victims. They are wicked men and women with no ethical or moral principles and vile disregard for life. Take a good look at how cruelly they pay here for the abuse and deceit they imposed upon these young women."

So spoke my guide, looking with contempt at the men and women in the oven who were on a lower level, unable to leave.

Oh, how wretched were those souls! All of them, huddled inside the ghastly furnace, moaned incessantly with no room to move. They cried, shouted, and burned inside without anyone to defend them from that horrendous punishment. All of them wanted to flee, but those who tried backed away immediately because the foremen of Vukub' Q'aquix were ready at the door, jealously guarding this accursed chamber.

Those tormented by the furnace could see the beautiful spring very closely, but without being able to reach it and refresh themselves in it. This further increased their torment as they saw the young women bathe and laugh, while they themselves were not allowed to cool off, even for a brief moment. In addition, the women who bathed in the fountain yelled at them angrily.

"Keep suffering, just as you made us suffer when you took us and forced us into a filthy vice. You deserve the payment, because it is your fault that the irresistible heat of your oven reaches us. Burn there forever you wretches! *Huya', chuya', pixhixh, palamuxh!* Stay there and toast, while we have fun here! Ha ha ha haaaaaaAAAAAAAyyyy! Aaaaay . . . !"

The laughter became "aaays" of pain because the fountain had heated up again. That was the punishment of those deceived young women. Sometimes they cried out in pain when the water boiled; other times they laughed when the water cooled down.

At those moments I thought about the current problems that plague humanity. Prostitution is nothing new, but among the Indigenous people this was forced by the Ladinos who came to dominate our peoples through conquest and colonization. All of our ancestors, male and female, had to serve as slaves to the powerful men who controlled our lives. Unfortunately, the suffering of the peoples continues in our day, and I think that on earth there is no place where peace and justice really shine. The world collapses under the weight of evil, and men no longer want to be builders but destroyers.

These present thoughts ran through my mind as my guides promptly took me into another room. The road was more passable and there were fewer cliffs, or snakes that crawled across our path.

9

THE LIARS

THE PLACE where my guides led me was dark, so dark. My guides were my torches on the way, for only they could lead me with safety through the dangers lurking all around. My eyes felt blind, and I couldn't distinguish anything among our surroundings.

Instead, my kind guides kept all eyes watching over me and protecting me from danger. They did not release me, because they knew I could not long survive in this darkness where Vukub' Q'aquix roared angrily.

Danger stalked us at every step, in addition to the traps and tests I had to pass to continue the journey alive.

As we walked, I began to hear chilling screams from afar at every moment in the dense darkness.

My feet began to tremble and my skin to bristle, as little by little the fear took me over. Just a few drops of force kept my body upright, and I don't know why I had to witness all these terrifying visions.

Seeing my steps slow and heavy with fear, one of my guides lifted me up in his arms like a tired child who no longer wants to walk. Thus they led me to that place where my eyes could see why those unfortunates screamed with such anguish, irritating the eardrums of hell.

As we arrived I could see the cause of these thunderous screams. It was an enormous line of men and women who were facing a large, smooth stone that blocked their way, a kind of wall. Many cruel demons were also watching over them from behind. There was no respite for these unfortunates there in front of the glowing slab.

My eyes grew moist as I saw the condemned souls beaten by their bloody executioners. All these people suffered here in Xiwb'alb'a, with nothing and nowhere to defend themselves against the deadly thrashing.

From the bottom of the room, a diabolical voice could be heard repeating: "One!" . . . And in compliance with this command, all the unfortunates put their left foot forward and stuck out their tongues to lick that great, glowing slab.

At that moment the contact of those viper tongues with the red-hot stone produced a scandalous noise.

Oh wretches!

Their tongues were completely burned and charred by the fire of the red-hot iron they all had licked. Like weary dogs, these condemned men and women had their tongues hanging over their chests, as if they were all desperately biting black, smoky rags.

Their mouths smoked, too, when they tried to lick their lips consumed by the fire. This made them wriggle and writhe in horrifying death throes.

They kept their tongues stuck to the red-hot iron until they heard the next command "Two!" . . . Then they took a step back, separating their tongues from the infernal, still burning stone.

Their bodies trembled, and they sweat torrents from the heat and excruciating pain. They too could not rest, for the moment they withdrew their tongues from the accursed stone, they had to listen with agitation to that fearful count: "One, two! One, two! One, two . . . !"

It was unbearable and endless, and the damned were completely overwhelmed. Even the bailiff in charge of this compound had an incurable headache from all his counting.

Meanwhile, the other foremen were shaking their heads to try to dodge the echo of the screams that bounced in their ears like thunder from an electrical storm: "One, two! One, two! One, two! One, two!" This infernal exercise went on and on, like the tail of Vukub' Q'aquix that never ends.

They had, then, to carry out the order without delay, because if they did not do so, the hysterical foremen flogged them with great violence, forcing them to continue the endless punishment. What great despair I felt to see them suffer and cry inconsolably. Their hopes were dead as they fell into the hands of their executioners, having entered through the dark cave door that leads to Xiwb'alb'a.

Though my bewilderment kept me from asking my guides any questions, one of them said in a penetrating voice, "Take a good look at these people. In life, these convicts were liars, slanderers, and false witnesses who made many people suffer through their gossip and deceit. Many people were wrongfully convicted and executed due to their slander and false accusations. Consequently, they have mortally sinned with their tongues. He who lies to save himself from some judgment or who points his brother to death, sins seriously. This sin is very frequent among humanity, so Vukub' Q'aquix is flattered to have many followers. This is the case of these unfortunates you see here, moaning and crying forever."

Thus my guide expressed himself, revealing the affliction for which these reprobate souls had to lick the incandescent slab.

Again, my guides insisted we walk quickly, for very brief was the moment they had given me to see that part of Xiwb'alb'a, the Siete Fuegos' mansion, Vukub' Q'aquix.

My fatigue was so intense that I almost felt unable to continue the journey; but encouraged by my wise protectors, I continued on my way despite enormous difficulties. My feet weighed so heavily, I had to lean on one of my guides to avoid falling to the ground.

They held me between them, and I took some strength to walk again. Meanwhile, the cries and screams of the damned continued to disturb my mind as if they were sky-splitting thunder, shaking the bowels of this place of nameless fear.

The most terrible nightmares any human ever had could not compare with these infernal visions I witnessed. Everywhere I heard terrible screams of agony, and laughter from Vukub' Q'aquix who continued in his arrogance, boasting of being the sun and the starlight there in the darkness of Xiwb'alb'a.

For their part, my guides never stopped encouraging me, instilling me with valor so I could keep witnessing these horrifying scenes.

My grief was also immense, because many times I thought I would never again see the light of day and return to my hometown. But Hunab' K'uh, who knows everything and can do everything, kept my heart beating and my knees strong so as not to bend before the cruelty I witnessed.

10

DESTROYERS OF NATURE

SHROUDED IN gloom, my guides and I continued with great caution along our macabre journey. Soon we came to another place where a wide river of turbulent waters was running. I stopped to listen to the chilling noise those infernal waters made.

It seemed to me as if millions of people were crying together inside that mighty river. Then, with my heart oppressed by intense and inexplicable pain, I said to my guides: "Let's stop here, I don't want to cross this river of sufferings."

One of my guides answered: "This wide river you see is the river of sorrows and despair. Its waters cry instead of singing, for they are formed by the tears of those who mourn for their dead and those who have suffered and cried for centuries there on earth. As you can see, there is no other way to go, we must cross this river you find so frightening."

And the other guide added: "Fear not, the oarsman who will take us in his canoe will appear on the other side."

I looked across but was startled to see large hungry crocodiles moving in the waters in the river of tears. No one could swim past without being eaten by these hungry reptiles, I thought. Not even traveling by canoe was the best way to cross this Xiwb'alb'a river.

My guides protected me, certainly, but I stood there trembling beside them, and panicking because the dense fog kept us from seeing even a few meters ahead.

One of my guides strained his eyes through the dense fog and spoke, saying: "The oarsman approaches, let us prepare ourselves!"

And so we went toward the riverbank, while the rower docked the canoe at a small wooden pier. With his oar the mysterious oarsman tried to push away the crocodiles following him in the water, under the canoe.

I got between my guides to board the mysterious canoe that was our only transport across the river of tears. So the first of my guides called the oarsman to take us very carefully to the other side. But the man did not answer, he looked like a ghost sitting in the canoe with his hands squeezing the two oars, which were of mahogany like the canoe itself.

Again, my guides asked him to transport us to the other side of those weeping waters. Then, after a prolonged silence, the oarsman spoke in his hoarse voice from beyond the grave: "We shall wait a bit longer, because others are about to arrive and they may also need transport to the far side."

My guides responded, "Very well, we shall wait."

We got out of the canoe and sat on a fallen tree trunk to wait, while the rower continued to sit in his canoe and wrapped in dense fog. We stayed there for a while until we again began to hear the bells ringing from the ground. Soon, the mist started to dissipate a little and we could see the arrival of two souls almost together.

The first to arrive was a man holding a club. He approached the riverbank with tears in his eyes and began to tremble with fear when he saw the hungry crocodiles moving in the waters. Seeing that he could not cross in any way, the man approached the mysterious oarsman and said: "I am traveling, and I want to pass to the other side of the river."

As always, the rower remained silent, without responding. And the newly arrived man begged again to be taken to the other side.

"This place gives me fear. Please, take me to the other side of this river that cries blood."

At these entreaties, the rower scanned a large name book and silently read something written next to the newcomer's name. Meanwhile, the strange traveler kept insisting that they take him to the other side, so the rower answered him in a hoarse and sharp voice, "I cannot, your name appears on the list of abusers of nature."

"That's not true," said the man, trying to lie.

"I have the list here and you appear as a heartless hunter."

Then the man began to cry bitterly, because he thought he was going to be lost there, eternally.

The oarsman approached him and asked in that hoarse, after-life voice.

"Did you have a dog on earth, and did you treat him well?"

"Yes, I had a dog that was a very good hunter," replied the man.

"Then call your dog for help. If you treated him well, he will transport you to the other side of the river. But if you treated him badly, the dog will not help you and you will stay here forever lost."

Very frightened, the man started screaming, calling his dog: "Witzitzil, Witzitzil!"

A yellow dog appeared and came running toward that desperate man. But he saw that his master had a stick in his hand, and the dog stopped abruptly as if afraid the man was going to hit him.

Seeing that the dog kept his distance and wasn't happy to see its owner, that traveler beyond the grave ordered him: "I want you to carry me across the river on your back, because I don't want crocodiles to eat me. I'm so scared!"

"I'm very sorry master, I can't get you across the river. How can I take you if you treated me very badly back on earth? Because of you, I endured hunger and thirst; after hunting paca, deer and other animals that you ordered me to chase and kill, you didn't give me any of that food. You only threw bones that were sucked and meatless on the ground, and you did not care if I ate or not. Also, if I got too close to the kitchen, you always had a stick by your side to beat me and put me outside, even if it was raining. Master, I'm so sorry, I can't help you because your heart was very hard on me," the dog replied.

Hearing that his own dog refused to help him, the man began to cry uncontrollably. There he would have to remain lost forever, unable to cross the river and continue on his way to the place of rest or eternal suffering. There, the punishment was to cry and cry forever, increasing the waters of that infernal river.

Then there arrived the other man whose journey to the grave had been announced by the bells back on earth. This disoriented man or spirit approached the oarsman and asked to be transported to the other side of the river: "I need to cross this river of tears to continue my journey. Could you transport me to the other side?"

As always, the oarsman didn't answer right away. Afraid that he hadn't been heard, the traveler insisted, "Please, I need to cross to the other side of the river in the canoe, because I'm terrified of those crocodiles in the water."

"I cannot take you to the other side of the river without knowing if you treated animals well there on earth," the oarsman responded, yawning with boredom.

"Yes, I treated them very well," said the man with his voice full of hope.

"Very well, we'll see if what you say is true."

Saying this, the oarsman began to review the book to find the name of that newly arrived traveler. He flipped through the pages quickly and finally stopped by putting his finger on the name. Then he looked at the man and said, "It is true, your name is not among the abusers of nature. But yes, here is a note accusing you of minor misconduct due to your carelessness. It is nothing serious, so you may continue your journey."

This made the newly arrived man happier, and he asked again, "And now, how must I cross to the other side of the river?"

"If you had any dogs there on earth, call them so that they may help you to cross."

Without waiting more, that traveling spirit began to name one of his dogs who had already died and whom he had loved dearly there on earth.

"Kamil, Kamiiiil!" he called, and soon a large, wolf-like dog came to help him. Seeing his master, the dog was on top of him, licking and wagging his tail with great joy.

"How wonderful to find you here, dear friend! Now, I want you to help me get to the other side of this river. I'm afraid to cross it because its waters are full of hungry crocodiles," said the man.

"Master, don't be afraid. Get on my back and hold on to my ears because I'll quickly swim you to the other side," the dog replied, wagging his tail happily. "You treated me very well back on earth. You fed me, you pet me a lot, and when I did some hunting for you, you shared your food with me. For having treated me very well, I would like to help you cross this river of death. Get on my back and do not bend over to see the crocodiles, because you can get very scared and fall into the water where I can't rescue you."

Saying this, the dog allowed the man, or spirit, on his back, and then the dog jumped into the water, swimming quickly and dodging the crocodiles that wanted to eat the man and his dog.

Upon reaching the other side, the dog shook the water from his body and led his master on down the mysterious road of *kamb'al*, the place of death.

My guides were satisfied to see my reaction. I understood immediately that dogs also have their animal spirits. Even in that other life, the dogs will remain faithful to their masters if they were treated well there on earth. If people who abuse animals observed what I had just seen, they would change their attitude towards these defenseless beings. Today, there on earth, men mistreat animals, especially dogs, and are not aware of the great help that these animals give to humanity.

After some time of reflection, my guides either spoke to me or woke me up, saying, "It pleases us greatly that you have understood the need to be compassionate towards dogs and other creatures of nature. Everyone who does good there on earth has their reward here in the afterlife. And not only with your fellow people, but also with animals and nature with which humans share their existence there on earth."

I was happy to see the man reach the other side of the river with the help of his dog. Then my guides asked the oarsman to take us over in the canoe. I was still a living soul, and they didn't use the dog test on me. The rower waved us into the canoe, and we crossed.

As the three of us sat in the canoe, the oarsman, without speaking, began to row, entering the dark mist that enveloped us. Little by little, the atmosphere cleared up as we approached the other side of the great river of tears.

Upon reaching the shore, the rower stopped at a small wooden pier and there motioned for us to get off. My first guide came down and held out his hand to help me down, for under the canoe the great hungry lizards still lurked. It seemed to me that this was the main path that souls would take upon their arrival at *kamb'al*, the place of death. Everyone has to pass this river of tears, then take the path of fear to reach the large gate that only prayers can open. This made me think we were emerging from the depths of Xiwb'alb'a.

After crossing the river, my guides ordered that we continue on our way more quickly. Fortunately, the scenes I would now see were no longer as disturbing as those I had witnessed further down in the depths of Xiwb'alb'a. Now I was in better spirits, for I felt sure we were rising to the surface of that realm of eternal pain.

We walked a bit along the bank of the river of tears and soon arrived at a great plain.

"This is the valley of waiting," said one of my guides. "All those who crossed the river and who bore the sign of abuse against nature on their hands are gathered here to witness their own destructive acts. Before continuing, we shall see what happened to the man who crossed the river with the help of his dog."

Indeed, I felt curious to know what had been the end of that man who crossed without difficulty on his dog's back. He had already passed the test of the river of tears and was now waiting together with others to be led to the Door of Prayer.

We got closer to the valley of waiting, where a crowd had gathered. Everyone here had been found with a notification next to their names as nature abusers.

Here that man along with many others huddled on the edge of a great circle of flaming fire. The heat reached those unfortunates, who sweated profusely without being able to leave. They tried to defend themselves from the flames that the burning trees produced, while asking for water to quench their thirst.

"Why does that man suffer together with the others, if he was able to cross the river and had treated his dogs well?" I asked upon seeing how he suffered, though it was moderate compared to what I had seen earlier.

"Men who hunt animals, even to feed their families, also sin against nature. Some hunt and kill animals without worrying if that species is facing extinction. The good hunter must follow and comply with the rules imposed by your ancestors. Before going hunting, the man should pray and ask the forest keeper to give him a deer, a paca, a rabbit, or whatever. But first, the hunter must apologize for the damage and death he will cause to an animal, which he will then use to feed his family. The Creator has provided humanity with everything for its subsistence, but in the same way, there are rules to follow so as not to abuse the right to live of other beings. This man, then, killed more than necessary, and that is why he is here waiting with the other abusers of nature. In addition, this man, like many of those gathered here, started a fire by mistake when he was cultivating the cornfields"—answered one of my guides.

The man was sitting on the edge of that great burning forest, along with others who suffered from the overwhelming heat and thirst. Then, I was surprised to see this hunter's wolfdog, the same one that had transported him to the other side of the river, come running to his master's side, his body soaked in water. The dog stood next to his master and shook the cool water from his body to refresh him. The man felt a great relief when his dog shook off the water and it fell on him like a cooling drizzle. The dog kept coming back to refresh his master, always wagging his tail as a sign of gratitude for good treatment. The others envied the fate of this man, as they too wanted a dog to help cool them from the unbearable heat.

I realized then how special dogs are, that even in this other life they are of great help if they have been treated well on earth.

"It is enough, let us continue on our way, as it is getting late," said my guides.

We promptly continued our journey in that immense valley on the banks of the great river of tears. We had not walked much when one of my guides stopped abruptly, saying: "Look over there, there are the real abusers and destroyers of nature, those exploiters who accumulate wealth regardless of the damage they do to the earth or to nature herself. These are here condemned, and they do not stop working to destroy life and themselves. What they did on earth they are doing here too, although now as a punishment."

I climbed up on a rock and from there I saw terrible destruction. The beautiful forests and rivers were mercilessly destroyed and polluted. Inhuman men were there with axes, knocking down huge trees and destroying forests and mountains everywhere. They sweat profusely as they cut down the huge mahogany, cedar and conacaste trees, with no end to their work. I saw that the animals ran in fear, defending themselves from those destructive men, but then they gathered together and screamed, causing the same trees, their lair, to rise up again. Thus, those men worked and suffered, destroying the trees that crushed them when they fell; but later, men and trees rose to their feet to carry on the endless work.

At dusk, after working long hours without resting, the men were led by the Vukub' Q'aquix guards into a dark, cold room. But these destroyers were not satisfied with their given resting spaces and complained, saying, "It's too cold here! We don't like the cold! Get us out of here!"

Then the guards in charge of these souls ordered them to be taken out of the cold room and thrown into another where it was too hot. Soon, the heat intensified until it almost burned them. Then these men, or spirits, shouted again, saying, "Ay, it's too hot here! Get us out before we burn up!"

Once again, the guards of this great valley of waiting grabbed them and thrust them into the enclosure of intense cold. They stayed there for a short time until they asked again to be taken to the place of heat. So the guards stayed angry, kicking and whipping them from one place to another to comply with their tastes.

Then my guides let me know the reason why those unfortunates had to suffer: "The earth is the home of all living beings, and no one has the right to decide about the lives of others. Destroying the environment by accumulating wealth, to the detriment of others, has its punishment here in the afterlife. Man should take only what he needs. Furthermore, the earth, which is the mother of all, cannot withstand so much damage and destruction. One must be compassionate with it and maintain the balance and harmony that should exist between men, nature, and the Creator."

I considered the words of my guide, who spoke a great truth. Now, no one thinks like our ancestors who asked a tree for forgiveness and patience before cutting it down for some service to the community. The rule today for men is destroy and destroy, with no regard for future generations.

Time passed; without realizing it I had remained static, observing the punishment of these abusers with no compassion or respect for Mother Nature. I reacted when I heard the voice of one of my guides saying: "Let us withdraw, as we still have some length to go."

Complying with his request, we immediately walked away, leaving behind that place of suffering heat and cold.[*]

---

* Perhaps climate change is a similar punishment for mankind's destructive acts.

11

THE CURSED SANDALS

SUDDENLY. AS we were walking, I heard a terrifying scream, starting like a whinny then turning into groans of pain. "Heeiiiaa, heeii-iaaa, aayyyyyy . . . !" It seemed to me that those deathly wheezes came from some beast in agony. The noise frightened me, but it also made me curious to know who or what was making it. Without considering the danger I went ahead beyond my guides until I entered into chaotic darkness. Like a child attracted by something that catches his attention, released from the hands of his parents, so I went without feeling any danger.

The screams came from far away, and so, full of confidence, I kept walking into the dark. But when I was a few steps ahead of my guides, an evil demon overseer took advantage of my carelessness to capture me and drag me into the darkness. My guides ran to rescue me, but several of Vukub' Q'aquix's foremen opposed them, stopping them when I most desperately needed their help. I wanted to cry and scream, but I couldn't because the wretch was covering my mouth with his disgusting hand. My guides also struggled to get away from the demons who clung to them like mischievous monkeys, not letting them advance. The Vukub' Q'aquix assistant, dragging me along at will, took me to a room and there closed the door, locking it so that my guides would not enter.

Upon finding myself alone in this room, at the mercy of this dreadful guard, my fear overwhelmed me, and I began to cry like a child. I thought I was lost forever. My guides did not come to rescue me, and I could not get to them. Those pale foremen had already tried several times to entrap me, but my good protectors had always saved me in time. Now my carelessness had taken over, and I was like a trapped mouse, trembling between the hairy hands of this treacherous being.

As I was struck dumb with fear, I noticed that on the stinking ground where we stood a mare lay crushed, almost half dead under the weight of its heavy load. The driver, instead of helping the poor animal by relieving her of her load, was driving her with tremendous lashes so that the mare had to get up and try to walk under all that weight.

"Aaaay, mercy, mercy!" the beast shouted, bathed in tears. And as I remained immobile in such terrible company, my heartless captor addressed me: "Now that you have fallen into my hands, I will never let you leave. I've got you, I've got you! Ha ha ha haaaa . . . !"

Thus he cackled sarcastically, while I almost collapsed from the fear invading my body.

In those moments I still longed for my guides, thinking they could not abandon me now that I needed them most. My hopes for salvation gave me enough strength to stay alive in the hands of this perverse being.

This character's diabolical and penetrating eyes fixed intently on me, but I tried to avoid them because his gaze was truly horrible.

"Take this whip!" he told me energetically, handing me hooks with which he made the unfortunate beast of burden gnash her teeth.

"Lead this damned mare down the rough road, and don't stop whipping her or let her rest. Master's orders," mumbled the accursed driver.

Saying this, he again lashed hard at the haunches of the tormented mare struggling to keep up under her heavy load. With great sadness I watched, while tremendous chills shook my body violently. Frightened by the continued absence of my guides, I began to shout loudly for them to come to my aid soon. But that accursed guard was still tightly covering my mouth, thus drowning out my desperate screams. My weak, frail body left me totally at my captor's mercy.

When he saw that I flatly refused to be the unhappy mare's executioner, the muleteer raged at me even more: "From here, you will not leave. Place these thick, hard-soled sandals on your feet. If you manage to wear out the soles quickly, you can leave soon; but if you don't succeed, I'll keep you here until the soles of these favorite sandals of my master Vukub' Q'aquix wear out."

Saying this, the demon gave me a pair of sandals with thick and very heavy soles, forged here in Xiwb'alb'a from a rubber that seemed impervious to wear. I felt a complete sense of failure and desperation. How could you ever wear out soles made of indestructible material? For the first time I felt defeated, totally lost. Without waiting for me to put them on, the demon himself forced these cursed sandals on my feet. Then the executioner ordered me in his hoarse and arrogant voice: "Today, yes, you will do as I order. You will beat this mare until her ribs are broken! Hurry!" he said, giving me a strong push and a sharp kick to the waist.

I wanted to scream in pain, but I couldn't because he had me gagged. And that's how he threw me down, but luckily I managed to get my hands on the ground before my nose sank into the dirt where the mare lay. It was evident that this evil guard could hurl me around as he pleased now that he had placed those cursed sandals on my feet.

My God, save me! I tried to scream, but the words never left my mouth. My last hope was fading, so I began to pray and cry out for my guides. Oh, my dear guides, come quickly to rescue me from this demon! I was trying so hard to scream that finally I freed my mouth. The gag covering my mouth fell and without waiting any longer I continued shouting: "Beloved guides, hurry and save me from this wretchedness!"

I was still screaming when suddenly that blackest of enclosures was illuminated as my guides burst in triumphantly. Oh, how happy I was! I felt a new courage when I again saw my dear guides up close. They had penetrated as far as the kidnapper had taken me, circumventing all the obstacles his henchmen put up; and thus they had reached the place where I was held captive.

The wicked guard was surprised to see them again in his presence. And as if thrown by lightning, that hideous character ran backwards, fleeing the radiance that emanated from them. There he then remained, totally disconcerted by the victorious entrance of my powerful protectors.

I wanted to run to them, but the heavy sandals the demon had placed on my feet weighed me down. So my guides were the ones who ran to me, embracing me eagerly.

I felt life forces returning to my faltering body. Ah, what great satisfaction I felt having my guides at my side!

"Are you well?"

"Yes, but these cursed sandals that the devil put on my feet fill me with terror," was my emotional reply.

Hearing them speak, my troubled heart rejoiced once again. Ah, forever cursed place! Just from having these sandals on I already felt a tremendous sense of punishment. What would those who are condemned here eternally not feel? What other hope can those have who no longer hope to be freed from these hellish punishments? Even if they cry, even if they scream, still it hurts them; they will have to remain eternally damned, they will never have salvation.

"Look at that puddle," said one of my guides, and I turned my eyes toward where he was pointing.

Behind the mare that was still crushed under the heavy load, there was a puddle formed from the urine of that unfortunate animal.

"In this puddle," my guide continued, "you must scrub these sandals so they wear out quickly."

So he said, and hurriedly I went into that stinking pool of urine and began scrubbing the sandals, just as I had been instructed.

The mare was dying, and when she saw us come close, she began to speak in a woman's voice: "Mercy, mercy!" she gasped out, as if she were being strangled.

And in truth she was suffocating under the tremendous weight of the burden crushing her. But the wicked driver, thinking my guides would do something to save or help this unhappy animal, approached furious and shouting: "Get up, damn mare! Walk, you wretch! Arrrrrreeee motherfucker! Fyuuuuuu! Shoooooo, you cabrona!"

The unhinged demon screamed and hissed, while twisting the mare's tail so that she would rise under that heavy load. This soul-turned-beast was making desperate efforts to lift herself under the burden. Finally, the mare got up and began to walk like a drunk, staggering under such a heavy load, while the wicked mule driver whipped her to keep her walking with no stops.

For my part, I had almost finished wearing down the sandals of Vukub' Q'aquix that so horribly imprisoned my feet. Ah, bloody horror! If my guides had not arrived, I would have already died among this filth, but no; my guides would never abandon me on this cursed path of endless pain and suffering.

Meanwhile, my guides, highly moved by the sadistic spectacle they were witnessing, hastily stopped the mare's forced march by throwing the cynical, accursed muleteer aside.

"Oh, miserable and suffering soul! Stop marching and tell us who you are and why you find yourself more tortured than the others?"

As they said this, the devil still stood where they had thrown him. The mare, moving her long ears in jubilation, raised her head to look at them; but before she could say a word, she began to cry bitterly, expressing her eternal grief. After a moment that mare, or woman, spoke softly:

"Thank you for taking pity on me. I'm still alive, with a living body there on earth; but the spirit that feeds it is this unhappy one you see here. Not long ago I got ahead of myself, coming to this suffering while my flesh or my mortal body remains on earth. Surely right now it is freely satisfying its perverse pleasures, without even caring about the evil it does me. I am *tx'ojye-swi'* and my name is Xhepel . . . , the darling of those who enjoy the forbidden flesh there on earth."

As this soul began to tell who she was and what she had done, my guides called me so I could witness and hear clearly the weary words that came out of her mouth, dry from thirst and hunger. Precisely in those moments the heavy sandals that were weighing me down had been worn off in the stinking puddle, and thus I easily approached them to better listen to this prematurely condemned woman.

"I," she continued speaking, "am married. But almost every day I cheat on my poor husband. I do not mind sinning, nor do I care if someone yells at me that hell awaits. So I do carnal acts even with my own godchildren's fathers. I know we must respect compadres and comadres, but this doesn't matter to me.

"The only thing I want is the taste of flesh, and so I calmly make my body a source of money. Furthermore, I made a pact with the devil by selling my soul if he would grant me wealth that I could enjoy without making much effort. Up there on earth I enjoy ill-gotten wealth and laugh at those I make suffer. This, then, is the reason why they have acted in advance to impose on me the cruelest suffering; earth has no punishment my body fears."

After hearing these doleful words, my guides intervened.

"This man also has a living body on earth," they said. "It is convenient, then, that you beg him when he returns there to tell your perverted body of the terrible suffering you still suffer in life. Only then can you free yourself from this punishment and return to earth to occupy the body your evil spirit now rules. This will be, if your body on earth realizes and believes in the message this man will carry. You have the possibility to free yourself from the clutches of this wrathful demon and live normally again, since on earth you still live and can repent. On earth is the only place you can achieve forgiveness, if you ask for it."

As my guides spoke to her, this animal grinned broadly, revealing her large, decaying teeth. She now seemed content and let out a neigh of deep hope. Before our very eyes she took on a new breath, standing firmer, confident that her executioner could no longer do her a worse evil.

The guard or muleteer had listened attentively to the talk, and now became wildly enraged as if wanting to attack us; but he dared not, for he feared my most gracious guides.

The demon prowled impatiently, looking for the opportunity to attack us. He did not want to lose this poor soul whom he beat mercilessly. The damned muleteer was furious that my guides had now given hope of salvation to this woman or mare he had mutilated with whipping.

My guides remained as they were, thinking of some way to rescue that spirit who suffered cruelly before her time. According to my guides, it was possible to free her from that premature punishment, because her body still lived on earth.

Death had not yet reached her, so she had a chance to repent. She was probably abducted to the underworld before her time, just as had happened to me.

After some time, one of my guides spoke: "In order for the mortal body of this lost spirit to realize and believe in the message you carry, it is necessary to send it a visible signal; because stubbornness and unbelief are part of human nature."

When he finished, the other guide said to me: "Approach the hapless mare and slap her hard on the leg. The sign of this strong slap will appear engraved on the leg of the same woman there on earth."

Cautiously I approached and struck the mare's thigh with my palm. When I withdrew my hand, at the exact place of the blow my handprint appeared as a burn-mark on the poor animal's dirty skin.

This done, the driver became more enraged; but the beast no longer paid attention to the insults he hurled at her, for she knew positively well that she would soon be saved. Fortunately, she had someone who could help carry back her message of untimely punishment here in the domain of Vukub' Q'aquix.

Now I realized why on earth sexual intercourse between compadres and comadres is prohibited. The Catholic Church has so strictly forbidden this relationship because being a godparent is a sacred service that should not be tainted with sin. Furthermore, she had made a pact with the devil by selling her soul in exchange for ill-gotten wealth; that's why she was abducted to Xiwb'alb'a.

Long did we stay in this place, but finally we moved on, greatly saddened by this soul still suffering in life and tortured on that rugged road to Xiwb'alb'a.

The underworld muleteer who was driving this mare acted suspiciously, wanting to lead her hastily down paths where they would not be discovered. Surely, this soul was kidnapped and, just like me, it was not yet her place to be here in this other life.

My guides and I left this dark room with our heads lowered, while one of them said to me, "This punishment that you have just seen is given to the possessed, those who acquire great wealth without jobs and in a prohibited way. Some have made pacts with the devil by selling their souls in exchange for ill-gotten pleasures and riches. The devil can give anything that is asked of him; but alas for the one who asks! His spirit will become the property of the devil and he will surely be damned. This is what happened to the woman we just witnessed; she made a contract with the devil. She did not tell us the whole truth of her existence, but it is certain that she has sold her life in exchange for money, and this was the cause for which we saw her spirit so cruelly trampled. On earth, the people who make these cursed contracts get rich almost immediately, but this kind of wealth does not last long, as the heirs soon squander it in vices and drunkenness. Those who make a pact with the devil are indulged in all his desires and enjoy lavish material goods. But upon death, alas! These people who have sold their souls to the devil will die together with their wealth because everything the devil gives does not endure. It is only a deception, a clever trick to trap the souls of weakest faith."

These words made me reflect and think about what happens there in the earthly world.

How many are there in the world who employ deception, scams, and other artifices to gain money!

How many heartless men are there who exploit the poor and add to their suffering!

How many sell their souls to the devil for quick riches through trafficking in illegal substances, while destroying many lives on the way!

This is a new type of contract with the devil that will also have its punishment.

Ah, what relief I felt when we left this room where for a brief moment those cursed sandals had tormented me! I kept walking as fast as I could to leave this gloomy enclosure, while my guides continued to protect me like a disoriented puppy.

12

THE COMPADRE PIG

DON'T KNOW how long we walked, but suddenly I felt the urge to take a short break. My feet ached where the cursed sandals had squeezed me, so I asked my guides to wait for me while I sat down to rest. I untied my huaraches and began to rub my feet, swollen from pain and fatigue. My guides did nothing but wait for me, because they knew my body was failing and needed a little rest.

While I rested, the image of that mutilated mare came to my mind, and this made me remember a story of reincarnation similar to that of the unfortunate woman, or mare, whose suffering I had just witnessed. I closed my eyes and began to remember the story of the lady who encountered Witz, the lord of the mountain. He took her to the underworld where she met her compadre turned into a pig. All this came from making a pact with the devil, selling her soul in exchange for easy and illicit wealth. I remembered the story like this:

One summer afternoon, Malin X. was on a journey from Jacaltenango to her villages in Tierra Caliente to look for and buy fat pigs, as she butchered pigs every Saturday to make tamales and chicharrones.

The women of these places never walk alone on these mountain roads; but this time she returned to Jacaltenango unaccompanied, as she had not found anyone to go with her. After walking for a long time, she stopped to rest under the shade of some lush conacaste trees at the foot of the great hill called Palewitz. This was always considered a mysterious place where some people had chanced to encounter the owner of the hill. Those who have met him describe this character as a monk or a priest wearing a long black cassock; hence the hill's name Palewitz, or "Padre Hill." This lady knew the place very well and it caused her some fear to stop there, but she sat down to rest anyway.

So there she was, resting in tranquility, when suddenly an unknown man with a sly appearance came slowly toward her, interrupting her peaceful respite. This stranger approached with complete confidence, even smiling as if they had already met before. But the strangest thing is that this man called her by her name, which caused a great surprise; she had never seen or met this Ladino, or foreign man. The lady kept herself still as she saw that strange man standing there near her.

Seeing that the lady was speechless with fear, the man spoke to her again.

"It is you, señora Malin X., right?"

"Yes, that's me," she responded.

"And you're the one who kills pigs every Saturday in the pueblo?"

She did not answer right away, because she wanted to deny that she was one of the few women who killed pigs in the pueblo. After some hesitation, she said, "Yes, that's me, that's what I do every Saturday."

Then the strange personage smiled happily and said again: "At last I find someone who can kill pigs. Now, I want you to accompany me to my house and kill a fat pig I keep locked up there. As no other person around here can do such work for me, I beg you to do me this favor. Do not worry about the time, because the work will be very fast and I will pay you for this service."

The lady was still a long way from Jacaltenango, and as she had planned to arrive there before nightfall, she refused to go with him to slaughter the pig. But that mysterious man kept insisting, promising that if she did the job for him, she would get home even earlier to rest.

So strong was his insistence that she, though worried and afraid, agreed.

"Okay, I'll go to kill the pig. And where is your house?"

"My house is very close, don't worry about the distance."

"You have to tell me where because I don't see any house near here in these woods," the woman insisted.

"Ma'am, my house is in this hill. I am Palewitz, the owner of the hill in front of us," answered the strange man with a Ladino appearance.

Hearing this name, the lady fainted. She did not know it or feel anything as the man who owns the hill named Palewitz carried her inside to his home. When she woke up, the lady found herself in a huge house full of all kinds of merchandise; outside she saw corrals full of all kinds of animals. Palewitz's mansion displayed an extraordinary luxury as seen no other place. In this huge house were rooms full of money and wealth accumulated in exorbitant amounts. This underground mansion on Palewitz Hill, named after its owner, is said to be a marvelous mansion.

The lady followed the man to a pigsty where a very fat pig was sleeping on the ground.

"This is the animal I want you to kill, as it will provide food for this afternoon."

So said the strange man, or lord of the hill, as he gave the lady a sharp knife. Since this was her job, the lady was not worried about killing the pig, and she carefully checked if the knife was sharp. Then, between the two of them, they tied the pig's legs to immobilize it, readying him to be slaughtered. The pig was growling with a strange sound that seemed like a human voice as the lady prepared to kill it.

"I need some bowls to receive the pig's blood," she told the owner. Palewitz went to the kitchen to bring some large bowls to receive the blood. The lady was about to slice the animal's throat, when surprisingly it spoke.

"No, don't kill me, comadre!" the pig shouted in anguish.

Alarmed, the lady stood up. Was she dreaming? No, she was not dreaming. To be sure, she pinched her buttocks, and they hurt. How strange, a pig calling her a comadre!

As the lady stood dumbfounded, the owner of the pig approached angrily, ordering her again: "Kill him at once! So he won't communicate with anyone."

Only this did the man say, then he retired back to the kitchen.

Taking advantage of the opportunity while the man was not looking, the pig spoke again: "Woe to me, comadre, every Saturday they kill me like this! How I suffer when the sharp knife plunges into my throat! They will continue to sacrifice me all the time, making me suffer horribly without actually dying. Now that you have come to execute me, I beg you to help me. When you open my chest, take out my heart and take it away! Only then do I believe that I will free myself from this place of torture. If this man thinks of paying you, don't accept anything from him, because if you receive something from him, he will beat you too. When you take out my heart, take it and don't give it to him even if he asks. Please do me this great favor, comadre."

After hearing this strange plea, the bewildered woman asked the pig, "Who are you? And how did you end up here?"

The animal replied in this way, crying like a person: "Don't you remember me, comadre? My name in life was . . . A. X. My family was very poor, but I, full of ambition, accepted riches from the devil in exchange for my poor heart. I didn't have time to regret it, nor did I think I was going to suffer a horrible punishment like this.

Warn all the people you know not to make pacts with the devil by selling their heart to him. This punishment is as cruel as you can see, and I hope others do not pay for their ambition by engaging in illicit acts, selling their soul to the devil."

The pig barely had time to say or growl this before the owner yelled from the kitchen, "Eh, señora! Are you done with work yet?"

The lady replied timidly: "I don't dare to kill this pig! Better another day I come and kill him."

"Fuck doing it another day! Right now I want it for chicharrones! And if you don't want to do me this favor, I won't let you out of here either."

Hearing Palewitz's threat, the lady had to execute that unhappy pig. Deeply saddened and with her hand trembling with fear, she plunged the knife into the throat of the huge pig who had identified himself as her compadre.

When he felt the edge of the steel, the doomed pig began to groan or scream outrageously: "Eeeeeeee! Eeeeeeee! Eeeeeeee! Aaaaaayyyyyy!!!"

Little by little, the pig's deafening wails faded into low cries of agonizing pain. Finally, there was no more noise. The pig had sadly expired after losing his blood from the knife in his throat.

The pig's owner was ready, observing with a thousand eyes the lady's every movement. Very carefully, the lady took the heart out of the pig and wanted to wrap it in a napkin, but the master noticed and snatched it away saying: "This heart will never leave here. This is my property."

Seeing that she could not deceive him, she said: "In any place where they have asked me to go slaughter pigs, they have always given me as payment, the heart. In this case, and as the only payment, I want you to give me this heart to take home. It is the only thing I ask for the work done."

Palewitz fumed at this, and said to the lady: "Here, I am the only one who decides. I will pay you well with coins of silver, and you can take all you want."

As he said this, he raised a huge bowl to fill it with money and hand it to the lady. But she refused the money, saying, "If you want to pay me, give me the pig's heart. That's the only thing I want."

Then Palewitz became more enraged and said, "I have already said that this heart will never leave here. It is my property and it must remain in this pigpen forever."

Saying this, he threw the pig's heart into the sty. At that moment, when the heart touched the ground, suddenly there stood another fat pig identical to the one that the lady had killed an hour before. Without a doubt, it was the same compadre who lived here condemned and transformed into a pig. Poor compadre, this he had earned in return for a few days of joy in the first life. What a terrible punishment that was! To be sacrificed every Saturday to satisfy the taste of the owner of the hill who demanded his Saturday chicharrones.

The lady, who still did not know how she had entered this luxurious mansion under the hill, asked to leave immediately. She did not accept the money or riches that Palewitz offered her. The only thing she wanted was the heart of that pig, but this was denied. The lady was hysterical and demanded to be taken to the same place where the owner of the hill had brought her.

And so it was that Palewitz carried the frightened lady back to the village road. Without the woman noticing or feeling it, she was near Jacaltenango, the town she needed to reach. Not at all tired, the lady arrived at home as if she hadn't wasted any time on the way. Surely, that lady had briefly visited the underworld, and it is there that she learned the true suffering of those who make pacts with the devil.

Unfortunately, she hadn't been able to rescue the pig's heart and liberate her compadre from that horrible infernal punishment.

"Wake up, we must continue our journey," said my guides.

I roused myself abruptly and tried to stand up, but my knees buckled. Again, I made an effort to raise myself, but I couldn't, I felt dizzy and with a severe headache.

With great concern, my guides urged me on: "Speak! How do you feel now?"

I replied, my voice tired and almost stammering: "I feel I can no longer continue my journey. Please, I don't want to move anymore! I feel like dying! Pity me!"

Unable to contain myself, I burst into tears like a helpless child. An irrepressible sadness or longing tore my heart to pieces. My guides let me cry and vent freely, so I continued to plead: "I can't, I don't want to keep seeing this excruciating suffering. Now that we have come up from the depths of Xiwb'alb'a, I want to return to my people. Please let us return soon! My strength is weak and I long to go back immediately."

"Calm down, Antonio!" said one of them. "It is true you have become very pale and we see your body is about to faint. Let's go back down this narrow path, because if we go back through the door by which we entered, it is possible that the foremen of Vukub' Q'aquix will delay us with their traps."

Ah, what relief I felt at that moment! These sweet words were a flood of hope for me, because I truly felt faint and no longer able to remain in this world of pain. My body was feeble and my heart barely beating from all the fear built up inside me. My guides understood my weakness and decided to lead me down a short path or portal that passed near the entrance to Xiwb'alb'a.

To my surprise, the path we took was one that was rarely traveled, because only this way could we shorten the return trip. I don't know how, but my guides seemed to know all the paths of the underworld and all those that led to salvation. With a calmer heart, I followed my guides and protectors, for we were still in *kamb'al*, the place of death.

13

THE PATH TO PURGATORY

FELT MORE relief when my kind guides decided it was time for me to return from this macabre trip to *kamb'al*. We took another path to get out, because as I mentioned before, some short paths or trails connect with other levels or with the world above where sufferings are less than in the depths of Xiwb'alb'a. I barely managed to reach the third or fourth level, because no one alive could reach the greatest depth, the ninth circle where the throne of Vukub' Q'aquix sits.

We walked a short time before my body began to feel faint again. With great concern my guides took my hands and brought me to rest under the shade of some cypress trees. They sat next to me, checking the surroundings of those ancient trees by the side of the road. They were worried I might pass out right there, so they kept close watch over me.

After resting a brief moment, my guides lifted my arms and led me forward, saying, "We have short way to go and you must have faith in us, for we will bring you out alive from this place that frightens you so."

Then I directed my eyes towards where they were pointing, and I saw a light that illuminated the way more clearly. We would be climbing a narrow, dimly lit path. This gave me great hope and fortitude, and I felt strength return to my body.

"Come, you must endure the last stage of this passage," insisted one of my guides.

Meanwhile the other alerted me, "Do not despair, for we are at your side. Furthermore, we must leave here at once because the vicious guards are coming from behind with a beast that wants to ram us."

Sure enough, I began to sense the noise of the stones hurled at us by those hateful beings, eager to prevent us from leaving this damned subterranean realm. Then, before we could go further, the infernal beast caught up with us, wheezing furiously.

He was like a gigantic black bull who spewed smoke through his mouth and shook his head with those long, sharp horns. The fearsome animal circled around us several times but stopped short of attacking. He scraped the ground furiously as if wanting to tear us apart, but with my guides at my side, he did not dare come nearer. His trunk frothing with rage, the animal approached and withdrew, bellowed and sank his horns in the ground, frightening even his demon overseers who fled from his presence. Several times he seemed to consider attacking us, then finally he made up his mind. My two guides stood strong, and I, behind them, defended myself from that cursed beast.

The choleric animal, after scratching the ground, bellowed loudly and shot toward us. At that moment, a blinding light sprang from my guides, dazzling the murderous monster.

The animal charged towards us blindly, and so my guides managed to grab him by the horns and knock him down. There he remained, with his horns sown into the ground. It happened so fast that it seemed my guides had knocked the huge animal to the ground like a goat or some other small beast.

"Quick, take the cloth from your bundle!" one of my guides ordered, and I immediately took out the red cloth dyed with achiote. I gave it to one of my guides, and he put it on the back of the captain who commanded that group of accursed guards. Then, after freeing himself from the ground, the furious animal backed away, and this time he launched himself against those onlooker demons who had incited him, going after the captain with the red cloth on his back.

Satisfied with their performance, my guards brushed off their muddy hands and patted me on the back as if to say it had been no trouble. Certainly, with my guides by my side, I had no cause for worry, as they delivered me from any danger. And so I could relax a bit.

Being in that place of multiple torments put me in mind of all those who deceive their fellow people. I thought and thought of the evil of the devil . . . and I remembered what the Church has taught for centuries through friars and preachers. As a choirmaster and now a follower of the teachings of the Catholic Church, I understood that:

> The devil is a character detestable,
> brimming with envy, resentment, and hate;
> he who engendered massacres great,
> setting in motion the inevitable.

> He is the one to inspire the perverted,
> gaining adherents for measureless hell;
> with his great horns he will lead and compel
> those who will follow, the poor unconverted.

> This evil character, raging like fire . . .
> he the sole father of every liar,
> he who so fiercely the criminal meets.

He our most terrible, deadly foe,
thorns in our path he will ever sow,
misleading us with his fatal deceits.

One of my guides ran his finger across my nose, waking me from my deep lethargy. I awoke more serene and optimistic, and my heart encouraged me to live. I had drifted off to a little sleep or blackout from which I was now recovering.

Returning to reality, I realized that many Vukub' Q'aquix foremen had us surrounded. They realized that we were about to leave those gloomy mansions, and that is why they wanted to stop us at all costs. Their leader and the biggest one approached us saying, "Hey, you two! Why are you defending this cabrón? Leave him here so we can amuse ourselves with him!"

Hearing these words, I almost urinated from fright. What would become of me if my guides accepted such a proposal? Without realizing, I began to scream in fear.

"Beloved guides! Remove this filthy demon from me! Don't let him touch me! Don't let him take me away! I trust you, oh, dear guides!"

Seeing my despair, one of my guides gave me a strong embrace, protecting me from the threats of those accursed foremen. But the group leader kept urging my guides to hand me over.

"Begone from us, unearthly spirits! Or do you think you can thwart what Hunab' K'uh has ordered, blocking our way? Withdraw, for your threats do not scare us."

With these words, the one who had embraced me took a great leap, passing over the devils that surrounded us, while the other made them retreat with the force that emanated from his being. In this way we departed from that royal road that leads into the black depths of the abyss. My guide led me through the small gap that arched to the right, and here he kept me sheltered like a little boy. In a short moment, my other guide arrived, who was hurrying because the angry demons he had engaged were chasing him with more fury.

"Come quickly, these accursed ones are following us and we can waste no more time!" said my guide.

And so we ran on between gigantic rocks that hindered our escape. Behind came the army of Vukub' Q'aquix goons, with stones and clubs, determined to capture me. It was good I had rested a bit, as I needed to keep running after my guides along that unknown road to free ourselves from our pursuers. I could not fall behind because the angry demons were almost nipping at our heels as they yelled insults and vulgarities.

Thus I kept running like crazy, or like a fugitive, eager to break free from the poisons of those criminal devils who sought without reason to claim me. Nor was I willing to take a horrible beating from those angry demons, so I kept running alongside my guides. The accursed guards, aware of the terrain, were making up ground, now almost reaching us. Behind me I could hear their maddening screams.

"We've got them! They won't be able to escape the abyss! Hurry, compas, because we've just about got them! We'll enjoy pounding this wretch with our fists! They're ours now! We've got them! Heh, heh, heh!"

They kept shouting furiously behind us, while my legs became weak again and suddenly I fell crashing to the ground, as if struck by lightning.

My guides immediately picked me up like I was a passed-out drunk and dragged me away. Behind us the shouts, insults and threats accompanied by stones and clubs came through more clearly. They had almost, almost reached us!

The leader, the strongest demon of them all, was still at the head of the pack. What despair! Just to see them made my teeth gnash with fear. What would become of me if they caught up with me?

I could not bear to think about it anymore, as my insides twisted with fear. Our pursuers came closer and closer, and my heart was beating like a war drum. In these critical circumstances, suddenly we stopped abruptly before an immense ravine. Even my guides were concerned when they saw such an inconceivable abyss. What to do now in the face of such an unexpected obstacle? How to cross it if even my guides trembled when they saw it? I began to cry in despair, because I thought this was where my life would end. That's how I was, so desperate when one of my guides said: "Let us move on, for we need no bridges!"

With that said, we moved forward without looking down to the bottom of the great precipice. My surprise grew when I saw that as we walked, the edge of the cliff stayed ahead of us without our reaching it. The banks came together to form a narrow channel we could cross in one long jump. Without hesitation, one of my guides jumped, reaching the other shore. Then I jumped like a cat, and for a moment it felt like I was flying. Finally, my other guide jumped that very deep canyon or ravine. We did not tarry but kept running because the irrepressible demons were also preparing to jump the profound chasm.

I was surprised anew to see that behind us and with each step we took, the unfathomable abyss widened, until it reached the point it was before we crossed it. We kept running and running because now I feared that the immense ravine would open up behind us and swallow us.

Once that abyss was no longer stretching behind us, my guides and I finally stopped. I could tell that when we had started to run, the most daring devils who wanted to jump the abyss behind us took a dive to its dark depths. The others stopped as they watched their warlike colleagues disappear into the dark reaches of the abyss.

My guides had gone through the danger without much worry; I, on the other hand, felt my body freeze with fear. Had I failed in the jump, I would have been buried forever in the precipitous depths. But no, the holy hands of my guides protected me, giving me that great impulse that made me cross the abyss. They had been tasked to guide me, and they couldn't lose or abandon me when I needed them most.

It was truly mysterious what happened, how the ravine narrowed so we could jump. After reaching the other shore, the edges of the abyss widened again to prevent the demons from jumping over it as we did. No condemned man could cross it and escape these deadly gorges; well, there is a great separation between hell and purgatory, which I believed was the place we were now arriving.

From the other side we could see our enemies who had become far separated from us. They kept yelling and insulting, but to me their insults were already meaningless. We had gotten past their traps, and for this reason I felt calmer. Luckily we had left the limits of those infernal mansions. Now, the place where we were did not seem as dark as the one we had left, but it already reflected an opaque and slimy light that at the same time expressed a depressing sense of solitude.

We kept walking more calmly, because the accursed guards who had been chasing us were no longer there to throw their stones, sticks, toads, snakes, and pests at us. Left on the other side of the abyss were those cursed ministers of Vukub' Q'aquix who supervised with fury and fire the nauseating depths of Xiwb'alb'a.

14

AN UNEXPECTED ENCOUNTER

W E HAD walked for quite some time in this desolate region when in the distance I observed a small town whose houses were white with a soft and dim light. It moved my soul to see this town that looked like any Indigenous community in the earthly world.

"We go toward there," my guides told me, pointing to the little town I saw in the distance.

With no hesitation and with complete confidence, I followed the path with them, since I did not sense any more dangers like those we had left behind.

So excited was I to see this beautiful town that I rushed ahead to be able to rest in the corridor of one of its thatched houses. Many people gathered when they saw us arrive and they waved to me, welcoming me. Among all these were some who knew me, because from far off I heard them say, "Look, here comes Antonio. I hope he stays here among us."

Those who knew me very well approached hastily, eager to help me. They offered jícaras of pozol to quench my thirst. But, as much as they tried to offer me anything, I could not receive or accept it, for I did not want to stay among them, and my guides had strictly forbidden me.

Seeing how they insisted I eat or drink what they were offering, my guides told them very calmly, "If you know this man and want to show your appreciation, offer him nothing, because he still lives and must return to the Earth. He was only allowed to tread in these places for a brief moment, and with a strict order to receive nothing from the souls that dwell here. Let him pass and do not grow angry if he declines your presents, for if he did so, he could no longer return from whence he came. This, then, is the order that has been given him, and with it he must comply."

Thus spoke one of my guides to all these people who curiously watched me, without imagining that I still lacked their condition.

The people who had gathered to see me then departed without offering me their gifts or their bowl of ground corn. Some women seemed angry over not being able to speak to me at this time, as my guides kept pushing their way through them. Others, seeing me and knowing that I still had a chance to return to earth, began to mourn sadly, perhaps remembering their relatives or remembering the passages of their life back in the earthly world. Some cried, others gave out long sighs, as if they were very tired from so much waiting or thinking. Sadness and desolation showed on everyone's faces, although none seemed to suffer much. They looked like grieving children waiting for their absent parents. Their sorrows infected the atmosphere such that it too seemed to cry. Everything around them looked gray, sad and drab.

Then from among the multitudes, an old woman hurried forward and tenderly spoke to me: "*Wunin, wunin, kaw chin tzala hach wilnian!* My son, I am very happy to see you! And how I wanted to talk with you!"

These words of emotion and sorrow got me crying too. I had never before met this old woman who spoke so sentimentally to me. I was stuck there, listening to her sweet words.

"My son, every year, for the feast of All Saints, I have come to the house and wanted to speak with the whole family; but I don't know what is wrong with them. Or is it that they no longer hear what I say? During that time of permission which all souls are given to go for a walk in the world we come from, I was happy to see on the altar that they always put fruits, food, and candles for us. Although the candles sustain us the most, we always take in the aroma of what they put on the tables to remember our days of life on earth."

While she was talking to me like this, another group of ladies approached, smiling and looking at me with sweet approval. They nodded affirmatively, while the old woman continued to speak to me.

"I have also seen that those of my family no longer follow the good customs of our culture and traditional spirituality. The people are forgetting the traces of our ancestors and have scorn for our progeny. What is happening distresses me greatly, because respect for life and nature is being lost among the youth. Now that you can hear me, tell them to think of Hunab' K'uh, the One-True-God. Hunab' K'uh is the only light to guide our lives. He is the truth. He is the glory. He is the beginning and the end of the universe. Why be fooled by others?"

After hearing her pleading words, I asked her:

"Oh! old woman who treats me so kindly, tell me: Who are you? And why do you know me?"

"I am your grandmother, your mother's mother, and my name is Kantel. Truly, you didn't know me because you were still very young when they gathered me from that world. Oh my dearest boy! How much I remember you all, as I do that beautiful town of Xajla', Jacaltenango!"

Saying this, she began to cry uncontrollably. And I, deeply moved, approached her and embraced her tightly. Then I shouted with joy:

"Abuela, my dear abuelita! Granny dear! What great satisfaction it gives me to meet you!" Then I continued, asking, "Why are you in this desolate and sad place, where none of those present have any joy? What is happening with them?"

"We are in the valley of lamentation and hope. Our mind is serene because soon we hope for eternal salvation. Our punishment is still very harsh, because we cannot yet contemplate our Creator. We still have many sins to purge to achieve the eternal happiness we have been promised. As you can see, on our waists we wear these black girdles, which indicate that we are purging our sins, since we are not yet completely clean of our venial transgressions. But from the Lord's mansion, there, where lives true happiness, from there we can hear songs of praise that reach our ears to give us more encouragement to endure our purgatory. We are, then, souls with hopes of salvation."

After hearing her forced words, I hugged her again, while I said to her in a breaking voice, "My grandmother! In this happy hour when I meet you, my heart overflows with the joy that endures; and from this day, my eyes will carry your figure engraved, and I will remember you forever in my prayers. Also, oh dear grandmother, I will convey your good intentions to the family, as you still care so much for us. Upon my return I will speak with them, and together we will pray to the Virgin of Candelaria, patron saint of the town, to intercede for you."

After listening to me, her eyes clouded with joy and excitement. Then several tears rolled down her withered cheek, which I wiped away with my shirt sleeve. Then I questioned her again:

"Do you suffer a lot here?"

"No, we don't suffer even the slightest bodily pain. We have already gone through some pain, and in this state we find ourselves in, we don't even suffer from colds," she answered, with more confidence.

"Why, then, do they look so sad? Why don't they smile?"

"Ah, we can't smile yet," she replied. "When we want to do so, it brings forth tears. Our worst suffering is we cannot participate in the happiness of those we hear singing far away, and we are unable to contemplate the face of our Redeemer. We neither suffer, nor laugh. We only wait patiently for the day of our full and final salvation. The gloom and sadness of sin come to us still, but our salvation is secure. So here we stay without complaining, fulfilling the holy will of Hunab' K'uh, the King of Heaven."

"We must withdraw now, say goodbye," ordered my guides.

In compliance with this order, I gave my last embrace to this old woman with the black girdle, my maternal grandmother. But she desperately kept clinging to me to keep talking; I, against my wishes, became deaf to her cries.

"¡Wunin, machach toyih wunin! Don't go, my dear son!"

My poor grandmother kept crying out desperately. I even wished I hadn't seen her because it hurt so tremendously to leave her alone. But I couldn't stay with her for all time either. The minutes of my stay were numbered, and so I withdrew from this little community, sadder still by the unanswered cries from my ever-hopeful grandmother.

The others gathered there were sorry to see I was leaving. They all wanted to talk to me, but time was short, and I couldn't attend to all of them or listen to their sad sentiments. Only those I knew well had confidently come to tell me their concerns. Almost everyone wanted the same thing, that I would tell their relatives to remember them in their prayers year after year, and that they would not totally forget about them, because they still needed their help to reach the final goal.

We walked faster, as the road was more passable, although, as I said before, I found the atmosphere sad, gloomy, and desolate. It was only the hands of my attentive guides that led me on a safe path. I depended on them and had to follow where they kindly led me. My body was somewhat calmer and my mind more clear. The affection I felt from meeting my late grandmother made me forget for a moment the sufferings of the trip. In this condition I followed my loving guides, quiet as a sleepwalker.

FIGURE 3 The houses of Jacaltenango during this period. Photo by Oliver La Farge, 1927.

15

THE ARRIVAL OF ONE RECENTLY BORN

SOMEWHAT CALMER now, I continued walking between my guides who seemed never to tire. I, on the other hand, wanted to finish soon with this unsettled journey that had so completely exhausted me. But my guides kept walking without a word, and I was very well protected in the middle.

As we walked along those desolate roads, a laconic peeling of bells began to reach my ears, indicating a death. The *tan, tan, tan, tan, tan, tan* . . . !, persistent, monotonous sound of a bronze bell could be heard in the distance, and it made me suppose it was a child who had died, and they were burying there in the ground. Once again, my heart filled with melancholy when I heard the bells tolling for the dead, while I was here in *kamb'al*, the place of death.

In my town it was a custom that when a person died, the body had to go to the church to be blessed; and then taken to burial in the cemetery. Those bells reached my ears and gnawed at my heart with nostalgia, producing a great desire to cry. I didn't know why, but those bells touched my soul, overflowing me in a torrent of tears. I repeat that the tolling of the bells in the village when someone dies can be heard here in this other life, but very soft and full of melancholy. With teary eyes and a heart flooded with the sorrow of those death tolls, I stopped on the road, full of thought.

"Hurry, we must witness the arrival of this newborn child to the rightful place," said my guides.

It was thus that my guides spoke to me again. And saying this, we hurriedly walked towards the place where this baby was due to arrive. We reached in time to see the little boy appear, carried in the arms of a man clad in white. Three other men in white accompanied him. I was up close and did not take my somnolent eyes off this mysterious entourage. Attentively I followed each movement of those who carried the newborn in their arms. The baby was, I estimated, about five months old, and he was crying innocently in the arms of the man who carried him.

They stopped next to a large, smooth, concave stone that looked like a huge grinding stone worn down at the center. Then, two men stood at each end of the enormous slab, as it gave off fiery sparks. This stone radiated heat, which we could feel refracting all around us.

As I contemplated this astonishing scene, suddenly I was horrified to see that the man carrying the tender child in his arms rolled it naked onto this burning rectangular stone. When the tender and delicate body touched the incandescent slab, a whitish smoke rose as if the baby had evaporated.

In that moment also came a painful squeak like the noise when a frozen tamale rolls onto a hot comal, fast and loud as ice water poured through sizzling butter. *Tzzzzzzzzz . . . !* went the noise this little body produced as it rolled on the purgative plate that seemed to evaporate it.

The baby was sobbing desperately, emitting tender cries of pain. Oh, such agony for this weak and defenseless little body! A child at this age, with his material body, would not have endured such an ordeal back on earth. And thus the spirit of the newborn was transmuted from original sin to eternal life through this great burn-ing and purifying stone.

The boy rolled to the other end of the hot slab. Those waiting there gave it another push, rolling it a second time. When the child reached the starting point again, those who were waiting said, "Last turn . . . !" and they rolled him again.

Strongly moved, I contemplated this baby being punished so severely.

During the trajectory of this last roll, the newborn's little body was clearly transforming. Upon reaching the end of the stone, the purge ended, and those who were there joyfully received in their hands a little angel beautifully dressed in white. He had grown tender wings and no longer looked like the human body of before; he was now a cherub.

Only a brief moment did they contemplate him and caress him in their arms, as he immediately flew like a white dove flapping happily towards the eternal mansion of the Creator. Meanwhile, I was amazed by this painful yet glorious transfiguration I had witnessed. A beautiful event I will never forget!*

Seeing me so full of thought, my guides spoke to me as follows: "We know that what your eyes have just witnessed is puzzling you. And to dispel your cloudy thoughts and your doubts, we will tell you the reason. This child, as you may have noticed, took only a few days to go to the underworld. Therefore, he has no fault, nor has he sinned of his own free will. His parents gave him the proper baptism, erasing his original sin and opening the gates of heaven for him. But the reasons why this child, despite his tender age, had to purge are: first, because of the pain he caused his mother during pregnancy and childbirth. Later, like children at birth and during

---

* In this beautiful poetic fiction, the author has dispensed with the common theological doctrine: having nothing to atone for, this child should not enter purga-tory. Our poet wants to express the purifying and recreating quality of the pains of purgatory.

their early childhood, they have no awareness of their actions and get all their physiological needs in the arms of their mother, as it is she who sacrifices herself for raising her children. All these small sufferings the newborn causes the mother are also paid for here in this other life. So if a baby dies at such an early age as the one you have seen, and has been baptized, he will surely be received into heaven after going through this purgation. On the other hand, if the newborn was not baptized when he died, then the unfortunate would suffer much more."

Thus my guides spoke to me, clarifying why newborns were also punished.

It is such that the Lord's designs are so unfathomable and so just, that any little suffering caused to the neighbor will have its punishment in the next life. The same happens with any kindness or favor that is done for the good of any human being; no matter how insignificant, it will always have its reward.**

They spoke with me a good long time, and I, very absorbed, listened carefully, but I could not hold in my memory everything they said.

"Let us not waste time, let us continue on our way," my guides insisted.

And so we left this place where one finds the rectangular stone that burns and transforms newborns into little angels of God.

** Such as the case of the woman who instantly came out of the flames when her comadre called her to thank her for a small favor.

16

MAY PUNISHMENT FALL UPON THEM

W E HAD not yet walked far when one of my guides spoke in a loud voice, pulling me from my meditations.

"Let us see what that enclosure holds."

We went a short way over to a place illuminated by a dim light, which to me made it seem like an icy cell. We could see and feel an immense and contagious loneliness reigning there.

Upon entering this room, without knowing why, I began to sigh and fill myself with deep sadness. A tremendous anxiety and despair invaded my heart. Dense fog prevented my seeing things clearly and precisely. Not knowing why such a great sadness characterized this enclosure, I became terrified, and asked my guides:

"Dear guides, explain to me: Why does this depressing loneliness reach into my soul? I feel the crying could overflow from my tired eyes and I don't know why."

One of them, in reply, said to me: "Look, there!"

And so saying, my guide indicated something deep in the compound. I sharpened my vision and only then could I see, in the middle of the dense fog, a great number of children kneeling, posed with only one knee on the wet ground. With the palms of their hands together, they pleaded in loud voices something I could not clearly understand.

I stopped to listen to what they were saying, but the murmur in this dark room was so great I could not make out any of their words. They were boys and girls ranging from two to five years old.

All were locked in this gloomy enclosure, begging or crying out for something with their hands raised to heaven. Dumbstruck, I knew not what to do or say. What cause did these sad boys and girls have to suffer? My soul filled with great compassion for those unhappy little ones.

And so I stayed, almost motionless, but then my guides said to me, "Go closer, do not fear, for you are no longer in the mansion of Vukub' Q'aquix. Listen well to the words these children ceaselessly pronounce."

Somewhat cautious and fearful, I approached this group of little ones who were in so moving a situation. Everyone, with their hands together and their eyes turned to the heights, spoke in unison.

"Unfortunate are we! Why were we born to careless and unthinking parents? Why weren't we properly seeded into the world when we were born?* Oh how unfortunate is our luck!"

Others answered with an eternal litany.

"They will pay for what they have done to us! Punishment be upon them! May judgment fall on them!"

This and other things they cried, these poor abandoned creatures. I was speechless and saddened to see these children cry out for justice and punishment for their careless parents. Here were

---

* Referral to the ancestral custom in which the child is integrated as a member of the community; "planting the navel or spirit" near a water source, symbolizing enduring life and living part of nature. For today's Christianity, this symbolizes the cleansing of original sin.

infants and slightly older ones, in the same way moaning and cursing their parents.

"May judgment fall on them! They are guilty! They have done
us incurable harm! Oh God, in what abandonment have they
left us!"

Thus did these little voices cry out insistently, but their cries
had no answer beyond the echoes in that mansion. Their ills had
no remedy, because their ungrateful parents had forgotten them
forever.

After a while, I could not contain my tears and, with great dis-
may, I cried with them in their misfortune, sorrowed greatly to see
them suffer, so completely abandoned. According to their cries, it
was their parents who had placed them in this limbo, away from
eternal happiness. Immersed they stayed in this pitiless enclosure
where sadness and loneliness reigned eternally, while in the distance they could hear the laughter of other children who had
already crossed the great door of salvation.

"Ah, what soulless parents!" I thought to myself.

Feeling deeply moved, I went over to kiss one of the children
on the forehead, who was looking at me so innocently. Fully disoriented by so painful a vision, I went to rejoin my guides. Ah, if
only we could rescue those innocent ones from that place!

I could not fully understand why those unhappy children had
to suffer because of their ungrateful parents. Seeing me sad and
pensive, my guides explained the reason for this depressing sight.

"Know that these suffering children died without receiving
baptism. They were not in the grace of God when they died.
Among them, there are some already with the use of reason, others smaller; but they are all children whose parents refused to
sow their spirit on earth with the ritual of baptism, which is what
would have made them children of God.* These poor children,

---

* Diego de Landa refers to a ceremony of baptism with water among the ancient
Mayas.

they would like to see the Lord; but they still cannot because they have not been reborn. These children feel so unhappy and miserable that all they can do is cry out on their knees and with their hands together towards the sky; they ask for 'judgment' on their progenitors.** What is certain is that one day they will achieve their liberation, because they are in purgatory."***

So spoke my kind guides, while I felt a great whirlwind of pain oppressing my heart for those abandoned children.

"Let us not stop for long, because we have little time to depart this place. Try a bit harder to walk more rapidly," they urged me.

Again we walked, leaving behind those complaining and unfortunate children, crying their loneliness, waiting for the day of their salvation. Like a meek and fearful sheep, I walked alongside my strong guides, going from one place to another, still not understanding how I had come to this place of the *kamb'al*, the place of death.

** Among the Maya, the concept of judgment is that of punishment by supernatural force or God.

*** The poet here reflects popular opinion, but according to theological doctrine, these children do not actually suffer pain, because they are not to blame for their condition; they lack the happiness of heaven and live in a state of their own; they do not suffer, but neither do they enjoy the supernatural bliss of heaven. These are respectable theological conclusions and deductions. So, the limbo of children is not a dogma of faith.

17

THOSE WHO GO TO MASS AND FIESTAS

W E HAD walked a good ways when I saw in the distance a great line of souls singing to the beat of a melody as sweet as it was exotic. I stayed still, entranced by the celestial music those blessed spirits sang.

All who were standing in this long line were wearing white and walking, full of happiness. The line was endless, stretching off to where I could see them crossing the distant horizon.

Here my reaction changed at once, and a fleeting joy touched my heart. Unable to contain my admiration for the beauty my eyes saw, I broke into a wide smile. Then with more interest I asked my guides, "Who are those so full of joy?"

And they replied, "These blessed souls are on their way to worship Hunab' K'uh. They have already purged their sins and are now heading straight for glory. Come here and see where this beautiful line of joyful singing souls begins."

As they told me this, they led me by the hand to a place where I could better see what was happening. We arrived at the shore of a beautiful spring surrounded by plants and flowers of many colors. The waters of this wellspring formed a vast natural pool of extraordinary beauty, with a color of crystal-clear aquamarine. To my eyes, all this beauty was so exotic it could only be found here. The pond's surface was covered with foam as white as snow, a bubbling foam that looked like a blanket of ermine covering the cool water. Its constant motion produced a murmur of intoxicating harmony that left me awestruck.

On this side of the spring where we stood, the great line of souls continued, but those who made up this line were not yet cleaned, nor did they have the white clothes of those who had already crossed. Many were half naked and appeared to have been rescued from the clutches of some beast.

Then I saw what happened to those souls that came anxiously to the spring. Those leading the line looked disgusting as they entered the crystal-clear waters, but after crossing this foamy white spring, they were clean and transformed. Standing next to my guides, I could see how those who were crossing reached the center of the spring before submerging completely. Then they continued walking until they reached the other shore fully transformed, as clean as untouched snow.

There I was, contemplating this transfiguration with eyes full of rapture, while my heart also beat with a strange and irrepressible joy. How I longed to enter the spring of white foam, to join this line and discontinue living the pains of the world. But since I still had to return to the earth above, I preferred to stay still and continue to contemplate them in their great happiness.

"Take a good look at these people who have not crossed the beautiful spring," said one of my guides, bringing me back to reality. "They have finished atoning for their faults, but now they approach the fountain to cleanse themselves of the rot that smears them. They are now prepared to receive the eternal reward. As you can see, when they pass through this fountain, all iniquity is washed away. This is the fountain of grace that transforms them, the last transition to eternal bliss."

I could not make out or recognize anyone I had known. The faces all appeared ancient.

Who knows how much time they had spent purging their sins, and even in this hour they emerged triumphant to take part in the lasting happiness offered in the kingdom of Heart of Sky and Heart of Earth, which is the God of the universe.

Those who came out white after crossing the mysterious fountain were jubilantly singing songs of happiness, peace and triumph. They looked like innocent children, off to receive their first communion. From the distance came a sweet melody that resounded endlessly, while these souls sang to the beat a song of triumph and infinite joy.

To our lord in adoration
this hymn victorious,
sing we all glorious
in eternal salvation.

He alone can provide
redemption and grace;
we rejoice at his side
in his loving embrace.

I don't remember the other verses of the song, but that is how they sang this victory hymn, as they entered into eternal happiness.

I kept sighing and sighing as I watched them walk towards the celestial kingdom. Fortunate are they who manage to get into this endless line of clean and purified souls on their way to meet Hunab' K'uh, the One True God.

Those who filled out the other line, to await the most opportune moment to cross the white fountain, were singing as well, to a different hymn that went more or less like this:

Of sorrow we have had enough,
now we go with hope to dwell
in glory with no parallel
that offers us its love.

In expectation we do live
to follow the posthumous way
this promised grace that God shall give
that in his breast we come to stay.

At ideal opportunity
we arrive with voices strong,
and so, in blessed unity,
practice this triumphant song.

Beautifully they sang this song that was most agreeable to my ears, but due to the circumstances, I could not fully remember it either. These people were singing at the top of their lungs as if they wanted to be heard and attended to promptly. Every second that passed was an eternity that separated them from the final goal.

Here I stood as if planted, contemplating the two rows: one triumphant and the other awaiting triumph. The two lines happily sang those celestial songs, and their voices intoxicated my heart with utmost joy. The beauty of the singing fountain also infected my soul with an overflowing happiness. How much joy these souls felt, who, after so long being punished, were coming to see their Creator! They laughed merrily on the way to eternal life, for they already felt their foreheads crowned with the laurel of eternal victory.

After a while, one of my guides spoke to me again: "The souls you see here are those in a state of purification. These people were good. They did good deeds, went to Mass, helped their neighbors, and kept the commandments. But since man is imperfect, they always committed their little sins, and from time to time other larger ones, but they confessed and begged forgiveness for their mistakes. This is how they have come here without the deadly stain to prevent their salvation. Look at them, nothing torments them! They sing songs and praises to Hunab K'uh with great joy. These people also went to the village festivals to have a healthy diversion. When arriving at the towns during the patron saints' celebrations, they first visited the churches where they prayed and gave their offerings. In other words, they knew how to enjoy the things of the world by giving joy to their body and soul. They did not fully dedicate themselves to punishing their bodies for work. For them, life was a gift from God, and so they cared not only for themselves and their neighbors, but for all of nature or creation."*

While my good guide was saying this, the celestial melodies from the songs of triumphant souls kept reaching my ears.

"¡Mamin, mamin, Dios Mamin! ¡A' nimank'ulal jinhan!"

"Lord, Lord! God Our Father! Have mercy on us!"

I could clearly hear the voices of my people singing in Mayan, but I couldn't recognize them.

"Now come and see those who did not want to go to mass, nor to parties to please their body and soul in a good way," said my guide.

We took a few steps back and before me, as if some black curtain had been drawn, I could look down to those who, according to what he told me, did not want to go to mass, pilgrimages, or festivals.**

"Look at them, dirty, stuck in that rot that causes nausea and excrement. They did not want to go to mass nor to be distracted,

---

* Indigenous people speak of the interrelation between human, nature, and the supernatural or God as the appropriate way to live, respecting other beings that are part of creation.

** Mass is the ancient symbolism of sharing and joy in the gathering of peoples. The ancient Maya custom of *Hula'* (visit or return) or pilgrimage meant visits to the temples and sacred places of the ancestors.

and they punished their poor bodies with too much work. Among them are also those who said they never had time for anything; they were always busy. Look at them, alone and sad, watching pass through this faraway gap those who did know how to give themselves healthy enjoyment and let their bodies have some deserved rest there on earth."

My guide kept talking.

"These wretches would like to be among those who rejoice, but they will never achieve it. Their punishment is to contemplate the happiness of others, without feeling it themselves. This produces a cursed envy in them, which makes them utter grotesque words of hatred and resentment."

I was reassured to know it was only through a hole that I saw them. There they were so angry, calling out expletives and making gestures of spitting in my face because I was looking at them. Ah! With what sadness and envy did they see those who were heading for eternal joy.

I realized, then, that parties and healthy enjoyment are beneficial for the body and the spirit. Furthermore, events of joy or sadness we experienced in the earthly world are also repeated here in this second life. Too much sacrifice for the body is not convenient. It is necessary to know how to enjoy the gifts of life and not be too mortified, because what is done and lived there on earth returns in this other life.

As I had more things to see, my friendly guides took me by the arms and led me from that place where I had heard the sublime songs of those who crossed the exotic fountain. So, with more encouragement, I continued my journey alongside my kind guides.

18

THOSE WHO HELP IN COMMUNAL WORK

A FTER WALKING for a while, we came to a place where people were moving ceaselessly, as if very busy. They were all dressed in white and, as I could see, after working with great happiness in these tasks as they had on earth, they sat like kings to rest on large golden chairs.

With no worries they crossed their feet and relaxed calmly in comfortable armchairs. They wore red cloths on their heads like those used by the principales and alcaldes in our towns. These men chatted and joked without concerns of any kind. Among them were also women who happily held these honorable positions. Here there were no social differences, privileges, or discriminations. All of them had done good works, and here they lived in perfect communion, for all were equally valued, men and women. They all lived together without rejecting or envying each other. Ah, how cheerfully they shared their happiness!

Seeing such perfect harmony and solidarity among these people, I asked my guides, "Why do these people occupy positions of such honor?"

"These happy people you see are those who gave their time for works of community benefit. They did not refuse when people came by to request their collaboration, their help, and their service for the good of the people. They collaborated or contributed with joy and without protest, because they knew that the works being carried out were for the benefit of the people or the community. These, then, are the ones who selflessly helped in the construction of temples, roads, bridges, houses, etc. Those who helped the needy and affected in difficult times. In short, those who helped ease the pain of their brothers and sisters during famines and calamities."

In those moments I remembered the communal works carried out in my town in the past. Among the people here were those who had to build temples, forced to do so by invaders who imposed their religions on other peoples. Communal work has been a way of unifying peoples and resisting together any tragedy. This communal work is still practiced there with us, in my beloved town. For example, when the roof of the great church is changed, all the men gather like a party and selflessly offer their work to serve Hunab' K'uh.

In the same way, women also met and helped by making food to feed the men who repaired the roof of the temples, who cultivated the sacred or communal cornfield and who fixed the roads so that everyone could travel without problems. Now I see, then, that those men and women did not waste their time in vain; on the contrary, they acquired a good position in this afterlife. I could distinguish the old men and women of my town, who wore their typical white costumes. Those who did not occupy senior positions wore a red scarf tied around the neck or a blue sash around the waist, just as they used to dress in the town.

Here I saw some old men from my town occupying their golden chairs among so many people from other towns who spoke different languages. What an enjoyable and happy life these men and women had who had worked for their communities in their villages or nations. Serving God and serving the people is a mission of every human being, according to the ancient teachings of the *alkal txah* or sacred alcalde, and prayer-makers.

Then one of my guides spoke, pulling me out of my meditations: "Now, we will take you to see those who never wanted to help in charity work. Those who refused to help in constructions of communal benefit. Those who fled or hid when they had to voluntarily collaborate to solve the common needs of their peoples. See them there mourning and cursing their luck!"

They showed me a place below that of the good-hearted men and women. As I got closer I could see so many people fleeing in terror. No one was chasing them, but they ran like crazy, falling and getting up without rest. What they were running from I don't know, but where they went to was not a good path. They had to fight their way through brambles and thorns that ripped through their bodies. Thus, they exposed themselves to multiple dangers and pain trying to hide from the *polacos* or local police who blocked the roads so that no one would leave the town.

Then, I clearly heard what they were saying: "Let's run away so that no one will see us! Let's not waste time on nonsense! Others can do it, we have a lot to do! Come on, don't let those in charge catch us!"

So these disgraced ones screamed as they ran like mad to hide or find a path through the undergrowth. Unlike those who toiled with joy and then rested on golden thrones, these poor souls wore themselves out to evade community work. In contrast, those who did works, how happily they lived without suffering pain or worry! Here the work of all was recognized and they occupied positions according to their ability and knowledge.

Voluntary, communitarian work in service to the people there on earth is blessed by Hunab' K'uh, since it is the will of the people to offer their labor for the benefit of all. But obligatory servitude where the worker is punished and enslaved without payment is an affront to the Creator who has created everyone equally with the same breath of life.

Those who fled were totally different from those who enjoyed, because they were always running and fleeing, hiding in the bushes. These poor people were deluding themselves—by trying to avoid the service or cargo that every child of the people is called to serve with patience and humility, now they could never rest. This is what I saw with my guides, and then we hurried off.

We had walked not yet a hundred steps when my guides ushered me into another lighted room, very close to those who occupied the gilded chairs. I was ecstatic to see so many people experiencing such intense joy as I had not seen before.

"Come and see what's here," spoke one of my illustrious guides.

I hurried over to where they were indicating. I saw a group of people laughing at ease, flooded with much happiness.

Another of my guides spoke again: "These people lived well and respected their marriage. Look at them there very happy, without suffering any pain, because they were well married."

We stopped at a considerable distance from these who were laughing happily. Then my guide spoke again: "Look how the spirits feed themselves in this afterlife."

I stood still, watching them closely. Some large candles were burning, and the fire was also lit in censers. While the candles burned and aromatic smoke from the incense dispersed from the censers, the married couples began to inhale the smoke and with their hands pretended to bring it to their mouths. Others kissed the thick candles as if they actually ate them, but it was the smoke or the essence of the candles and incense they inhaled.

We stayed watching them until darkness came and night fell.

Then, those husbands prepared to sleep as they did on earth. In the center of the room they lined up the candleholders in a straight line, while the candles still burned, and then each pair spread their mat on the floor and covered themselves with a white linen cloth. Thus they lay down to sleep, so that the burning candles remained in the middle of each couple, separating them.

I don't know how it happened, but at one point I rubbed my eyes, and I saw with surprise that the people who had just gone to sleep had turned into little piles of bones on the white canvases. This was how they set out to spend the nights here in the afterlife, illuminated by candles that would never be extinguished.

I didn't have to ask any more, as my guides had told me that they were the "well married," that neither spouse had tainted their marriage and that they helped each other back in their first life. That man did not cheat or dominate woman, nor did woman cheat or mistreat man. Both in the couple understood their sacred service of procreation, valuing the equity with which the man and the woman complement each other. The woman was not considered only as an object of procreation, but her economic productivity was also recognized, the same as the man's. This concept was lost when the *uwes*, conquerors, and colonizers invaded our communities in the Mayab'.

I turned my attention back to those piles of bones in the light of the golden candlesticks. At dusk, those souls went to rest and sleep, turned into heaps of bones on the white sheets. Then, at dawn, those same bones became people who continued to enjoy the indescribable happiness they lived in this other life.

And so we left that enclosure to continue our tour, which, according to my guides, was about to end.

FIGURE 4 Communal work repairing the roof of the church, Jacaltenango. Photo by Oliver La Farge, 1927.

19

A BRIEF REST

Y GUIDES were walking, with me going slowly behind them, full of thought. I was so distracted that my guides had to yell at me to pull me out of my meditations. Maybe they had spoken to me before, but I hadn't even heard them. Then, very compassionately they told me: "Be patient, we have little left to go."

They tried to encourage me, but my exhaustion was such I could barely take each step. All my courage seemed to have remained in the depths of Xiwb'alb'a which we had walked through, and of which I did not see everything, only a part. Luckily, we had already left that place of horrible torments, because otherwise, the debilitating weakness in my limbs would have kept me from getting out.

My guides and I were going down a stony desert road, and the thirst and fatigue began to take me over. I tripped over a stone and fell face down on the ground, almost like I fainted. We were barely able to reach a resting place where an enormous cypress tree extended its shadow. At the foot of this tree were some large stones where we could rest. Overcome with exhaustion, I let my guides take me by the arms and sit me on a flat rock.

Here I lay down and lazily stretched out my body, while my guides reassured me saying: "Rest for a moment, for we see you are very pale. You can close your eyes and relax if you want, we will never leave you here."

So they spoke to me, while I closed my eyes to accept a dream.

I don't know how long I was asleep under their kind vigilance, until they woke me: "Get up, Antonio, you can't stay asleep here for long! Sit and look there in the distance where a large group is approaching, behind one alone who guides them."

I came to my senses, rubbing my eyes to wake up fully. Still exhausted, I pushed myself up from the cold stone where I'd been resting. Here I awaited the arrival of the group advancing toward us guided by someone who knew the way.

With great and resolute strides, those who made up the group advanced. To me they seemed very well dressed, and they all carried some old books in their hands. When they got to where we were, the head of this group ordered his people to sit next to me. We all exchanged greetings.

"*Hanik' wuxhtaj, wanab', k'ulnhem heye' teh yamanil.*"

"Hello brothers and sisters, I hope you are all well."

Then, the group's guide turned to me and said in a loud voice, "Your name is Antonio, right?"

"Yes, I am he."

This man called me by my name as if he had known me well for a long time. The guide was going to keep talking to me, but he stopped when we all heard the screams of a man who was following them. This poor man came dressed as a friar and shouted at the group saying: "*Mea culpa, et miserere mei!*"

Then he began to scream scandalously: "Aaayyy! Wait for me! Don't abandon me!"

I was surprised to see this man who came giving off screams as if he were desperate. I didn't understand what he was saying, because he used a different language first, then Spanish. What was clear was that this character came dressed in a black and torn cassock, and he showed a rusty cross so people would respect him and kiss his hand. But those of the group paid no attention to him, even though he wanted to identify himself as a friar by showing a cross that no longer shone, because it was lifeless. The friar had misused this symbol in his mission and now he was repentant, asking for forgiveness and mercy, but already too late.

In truth, this poor man or friar aroused pity and compassion.

He had a hard time getting up to us, and he stopped a few steps from the group. For some reason, the poor man didn't dare join the group; rather, he remained distant, as if ashamed of his own appearance.

The group leader ordered him: "Let us see, Tik Lanta, come closer! Come up here for everyone to see you!"

The friar tried to hide his face from him by turning back, then lowered his eyes to the ground as if avoiding everyone's gaze. You could see that this man was ashamed of himself.

Then the leader addressed me, saying, "I am the *ah-tz'ib'* Chilam Balam, the sage and diviner of the peoples of your Maya ancestors." As a chorus master, interested in the spirituality and culture of my people, I was flattered to meet the great Maya sage and philosopher Chilam. I was going to ask him about the Maya calendar, of which he was an expert, but I could not, because he immediately introduced me to the one who had arrived behind the others.

"Do you see this priest? He's thin and ashamed, right?"

"Yes, I see him, and I realize that he is very skinny."

"All those who travel with me were *ah-tz'ib'* (writers, poets) and *ah-b'it* (singers) just like you. I am Chilam, the patron saint of poets, writers and singers and other artists who have written to magnify their nation and salute the Heart of Sky and Heart of Earth."

I was flattered when the great Chilam Balam spoke to me, including myself among those who accompanied him. Later, the Chilam, the great prophet, continued speaking: "Look at these

KIDNAPPED TO THE UNDERWORLD   119

ah-tz'ib', poets, musicians, singers and '*mastrocoros*' who accompany me. They look strong and feel happy because they did their social duty well. They were not inveterate drunks, nor profiteers; they wrote to please, to warn, to denounce evil, to defend and teach others. I gladly accepted them, those of the word, as members of the group, but not this one," he said, pointing to the unhappy man who could barely stand before everyone's gaze.

"And who is this priest who is not allowed to be part of the group and who is ashamed even of his own existence?" I asked, a little more animated.

"This is Reverend Tik Lanta, or as the *uwes* call him, Diego de Landa. He came from the other side of the sea, not long ago, and burned and destroyed all the writings, histories, and literature of our peoples. He is the one who left our people orphans of wisdom when we could no longer use our way of writing. He wants to approach us full of regrets, but I have not wanted to receive him. This priest did a great deal of harm to our people and civilization, turning away from his true mission as a friar and bishop. Instead of recognizing the knowledge and values of our peoples, he discredited and rejected them, destroying the wisdom of our ancestors. We have not accepted him among us, and he is wandering with no consolation anywhere. He wants to follow us to ask questions about our ancestors, but we know that he betrayed those who gave him information before, and that is why we reject him. He has no right to be among us because he destroyed what we created. Just for you to see, that's why we brought him here. Now you know why we have presented him to you," replied the great Chilam Balam.

"Of course!" I answered promptly.

"Yes, I see you are reflecting on your life! You are a good *mastrocoro*, I know, but it is time to warn yourself about bad company and bad writing. Stay away from vices and false accusations. Take responsibility for your work of bearing witness for those who cannot speak out against evil. Sing Hunab' K'uh with all your heart, for that is why your parents made a promise that you would serve as a *mastrocoro*. We also advise you to help your parents, as every good child must take care of their parents in old age and help them bear their burdens. This, then, we have shown you so that you may try to do better when you return to earth. Everyone comes to earth to fulfill a mission, and yours is determined, you cannot refuse to serve with your voice and with your lyrics."

These words of his so touched my heart that I came to tears. I sadly evoked my past life. He considered me not so good, but also not very bad. In some things I failed and here I recognized my error. Then I decided to amend them and no longer reject service to the people and Hunab' K'uh. I felt distressed, since I had refused to serve the people as *alkal txah*, the necessary authority to pass on the knowledge and wisdom of my ancestors to new generations. This man knew all the little details of my life.

He told me no more. His words had been enough, as I began to regret the bad things I had done. Seeing me sad and worried, the great visionary and diviner Chilam patted my head for comfort.

While those who accompanied him laughed happily, the poor friar was passed to the front, looking distressed and disconsolate. Then he withdrew from the center to vomit and wipe his anguished tears behind some rocks. There he sat alone, behind the rocks, crying and playing with his rusty cross.

Then, taking advantage of this moment when the unfortunate man had moved away a bit to wipe his tears, all the *mastrocoros*, *ah-b'it*, and *ah-tz'ib'* hastily said goodbye to us. With their books in some agave sacks, the writers followed the illustrious teacher Chilam along that illuminated path without the poor, humiliated friar seeing them leave.

The group was already disappearing in the distance when he reacted and realized that he was alone. Seeing himself alone and abandoned, that enemy of the ancient word began to scream like crazy asking them to wait. He wanted to run to catch up with them, but he couldn't, for he was entangled in the dirty cassock that reached down to his heels. The poor friar continued walking, and on the way he fell and got up without being able to advance. "*Mea culpa! Et miserere mei!* Woe is me! Wait for me! Don't leave me! Have pity!" Thus the poor man who was despised and excluded from the group cried out desperately. The others did not care about his screams, seeming deaf to his unhappy pleas. With good reason, since the group leader had said he had no right to walk with them; for by his behavior, he himself had sought his exclusion from the group.

And so he continued his disoriented path, sunk in that desperate and painful ordeal. I became very distressed after seeing Tik Lanta. This friar was a *güizache* there on earth, one of those who write and bear false testimony, condemning innocent people to jails and torture. He used his writing ability to do evil, condemning many *ah-tz'ib'* to death, accusing them of being witches. In other words, he produced and elaborated texts, accusing our *ah-tz'ib'* of serving and being inspired by Vukub' Q'aquix, the devil.

This is how I realized that what is done there on earth is repeated here in the afterlife. I started to remember my past life, and some bad memories made me cry. Desperate, I returned to the place where I had been resting, and together with my guides we continued our journey.

As I walked, my turbulent mind stirred and recorded the words of warning the leader of the *ah-b'it* and *ah-tz'ib'* had addressed to me: "We are all born with a mission on earth . . ."

I had to speed up my steps, because the afternoon was already waning and we had to continue with that painful journey. The little rest had strengthened my body; in this way, I was able to continue the journey alongside my kind guides, who at every moment encouraged me to continue.

FIGURE 5 Main Street of Jacaltenango. Photo by Oliver La Farge in 1927.

20

THE RETURN

SUDDENLY, I began to feel that my body was lighter and more agile, less weighed-down. My steps were more constant and sure. We soon arrived at a splendidly beautiful place. Three elegant fountains adorned this wondrous and captivating room. The strange vessels were made from live logs cut to a meter and a half high. The upper part sprouted green shoots that, like a calyx, contained water fresh, pure, and blue, blue, blue . . . We slowly approached the fountains that were about seven meters distant from each other.

I was surprised to see that the first fountain was dry, as water no longer flowed between the shoots that formed a calyx of nearly dry branches. The water in that fountain had already been used and finished. The second fountain, the middle one, spilled a copious stream of living water. The water seemed strange and at the same time very beautiful. The place where the water fell was clear, spotless, and shone brilliantly. I turned my eyes to the third fountain, which seemed even stranger to me. This one was more beautiful and splendid than the previous two. The life-giving water that bubbled up did not fall to the ground, but rose like a sublime song to the highest level of the sky. In truth, these three strange fountains engrossed and enraptured me.

"What do these three fountains mean?" I asked my guides.

"The first fountain, the one that appears empty, is the one used in the past. Its time is past, and it is no longer in operation now. The one in the middle, the one that spills copious flow, is the one being used at present. Look how alive the fountain is! But when it dries up, then the end will come, and the third fountain will be used, the one that in the future will have a flow that is inexhaustible and infinite. As you can see, this is the most beautiful of the three fountains," one of my guides answered promptly.

With my limited intelligence, I could not grasp the true meaning of his words. I thought the symbolism of the dry well or of the past referred to what Christians call the Old Testament, and that the pool overflowing with living water belongs to the present, symbolic of the New Testament. The fountain of living and inexhaustible water of the future I thought to symbolize eternal life after the end of the centuries.

My other guide ordered: "Take this *tecomate* and fill it with water; that it will serve you there. Don't worry because it's not Xiwb'alb'a water and you can take it with you."

I immediately filled a *tecomate* with living water and took it with me. But while we were walking I could not see where the *tecomate* was, nor the water, despite knowing that I was carrying it with me.

So with deep admiration I withdrew from these three beautiful fountains to reach another truly dangerous point with difficulty.

"Now be careful!" my good guides urged me. "We will walk over a long, narrow stone wall to leave here. You must walk between us so as not to misstep and fall into the abyss."

And so I did. One of my guides moved forward and I followed behind him. Then my other guide followed me, so I placed myself in between them. Before my eyes stretched the very long and narrow wall over which we were forced to pass, since it was the only path that led out of *tanhb'al mul*, the mansion of atonement and eternal sadness.

We walked little by little as if on a tightrope. My guides and I advanced step by step, my feet unsteady and my hands trembling in the air, trying to maintain my balance. On the sides of the towering wall, echoes sounded from the depths of the immeasurable ravines, and suffocating fumes arose. I felt dizzy from looking down, but immediately my guides came to support me. Like a magnet, these abysses attracted or pulled me, wanting to suck me down, but I struggled to keep my balance. I did not want to die yet, and my kind guides made efforts to protect me and give me safety.

Strongly attached to my guides, we advanced as if walking on a thin cable. From the intense fear of falling into the abyss, I was bathed in a cold and copious sweat.

At last, we achieved the other side! I felt safe, and a deep calm entered my heart. Who would not be happy to finish crossing such a dark precipice?

I turned to see the dangerous and the narrow pathway we had traversed, and again a terrible chill invaded all my body. Alone, and without the great help of my guides, I would never have dared such an adventure. Only their protective hand had freed me from evil snares, and they had led me along straight, firm, and true paths.

I had not yet regained all my strength and spirits when we saw someone approaching, dressed in white like my guides. The man came hurriedly as if flying, because his feet didn't seem to touch the ground. Then he told us, worried: "What are you still doing here? Go back, for the time this man has been granted is coming to an end! You must return immediately so the visitor has time to get back to the world from which he came and occupy his mortal body again."

That was what this resplendent man had come to tell us, and he then went back with extraordinary speed to where he had come from. We also promptly returned, almost following in the footsteps he had made to give us the message.

Our return was also rapid, as my guides seemed to transport me through the air. So I did not feel the fatigue of returning or any stumbling on the way. In a little while we reached the large office where the great black books of life and death are kept. In a hurry, we presented ourselves before the manager or boss who had allowed me to make this macabre passage that now finally was ending.

"Well, now you are back!" he said to us all, and turning to me, added: "The time has come for your return to the living. But first, I want you to understand well what I am going to tell you and to keep my words in your memory. Be humble, but not humiliated, because your ancestors accomplished much. Try to serve your people, your community, and your neighbor as much as you can. You will see that people are not always grateful, but you have a gift, and you have to use it. You must also love and respect your village and your nation so that your actions are complete. Act according to reason, for only then can you return to enjoy the kingdom of Hunab' K'uh and not fall into the depths of Xiwb'alb'a that you have partially come to see."

There I stood, attentive to his words, as he continued: "Come here and see the mortal world."

It seemed as if he pulled aside a huge curtain, unveiling my eyes from a dense mist. Then I approached, puzzled, a huge window where you could see the whole world.

"Look there!" he said, shifting my eyes to a small spot.

What a surprise! I was looking on my town from that vantage point. My dear Xajla', Jacaltenango, the town of my ancestors.

But something among everything I saw caught my attention: the ladies of the Congregation of the Sacred Heart of Jesus. I saw them leaving mass. Then in the temple court they lined up before a large silver crucifix. They all carried white paper balls in their hands and threw them to the Crucified Christ. These paper balls symbolized the prayers or petitions offered by those ladies.

"Look well at what they do," the one who gave me the vision told me again.

In line, one by one, those women passed by, and from a certain point they threw their white balls of paper at the Christ. Some could not get their balls to reach even the feet of Christ. Others barely touched his ankles. Others got their white balls to reach his knees with difficulty. Only five of those from the great row managed to hit the side of the Crucified.

When all of them finished passing, the chief told me again: "Now you could see in what condition those ladies who proudly say they belong to such an exalted congregation are. Many are members of the congregation and go to mass, but not all comply. Some boast of belonging to said congregation and appear to be holy women before the eyes that see them, but when they get home, they are the ones who criticize their neighbor the most, the ones who despise the poor the most, and the ones who put their neighbors in trouble the most. In short, they are then those who failed to touch the Christ with their paper balls. It is not enough to pray and go to mass to save yourself. It is necessary to observe and practice the laws of God and also respect the natural laws. Holiness is gradual and requires many sacrifices. Those who managed to touch his side, those truly comply with religion. They are selfless, and everything they do they do from the heart. They are on the right track."

Seeing this, I was pondering. If this happens in small congregations, what will happen to large congregations, and in rich countries? I imagine that there is also deception, corruption, and falsehood.

This I was thinking when he, as if guessing my thoughts, said: "The same happens within large religious congregations. There are bishops, priests, and pastors who truly keep the word of Hunab' K'uh and are true saints. Have you heard of the friar Bartolomé de las Casas? He and others not only spoke out but fought for the lives and rights of the poor who were dominated by the conquerors. You also saw Pedro de Alvarado and Bishop Diego de Landa, right?"

"Yes," I answered. A chill ran down my spine as I remembered these suffering souls that I saw down in Xiwb'alb'a. I had also heard of Bartolomé de las Casas as the bishop who protected the Indigenous people of our towns. My people remembered very little of these characters who came from the other side of the sea.

Finally, he who had allowed me to see the gloomy mansions of Vukub' Q'aquix, said, "The terrestrial world is a beautiful place to live, and that is why you have to take care of nature as everyone's home. We must not abuse rivers, forests, animals, and everything that exists; nor should you abuse your neighbor. You must know how to forgive, for charitable souls pay love with love, while the vile and worldly pay tooth for tooth. Go then, and keep living in your village and with your people!"

Those were the last words this ever-blessed guardian said to me, and I trembled as I left that beautiful room, while the two who had guided me so wonderfully dismissed me with their deep, contented looks.

Suddenly, as I crossed the threshold of this enormous door, my eyes darkened. I could see nothing nor no one next to me. Now without a guide, I couldn't go on my way either. I was about to despair and sit there waiting for the dawn, but at that moment a little light appeared before my eyes to give me hope amid the darkness that enveloped me.

I could not see who was bearing it, and I could not speak, having lost my voice. It was then that I got up without a word and silently followed this small light that guided me through the dismal darkness that seemed like an endless tunnel. The one who carried the light walked ahead—or it was the light alone?—and I was following behind. Where were we going? Who was leading me? In those moments I could not guess.

For some time I followed this little light in the darkness that surrounded me, until dawn came. Then I arrived at a familiar place, and the little light disappeared before me, as I could already see my path clearly. I walked a little more and finally came to a straw house in the middle of a cornfield. The man who lived there was surprised to see me arrive alone. He was an old man who had lived in my pueblo for a long time, but he had gone to another village and died there without ever returning.

I asked him: "This is the village of Santa Catarina, right?"

"Yes it is."

"And why does it seem so changed, and with this pale sun that does not heat?"

"Because this is the Santa Catarina village of this other life."

"Ah, I can see that!"

It seemed to me I was in that gray level or world, where the pale-faced man I described at the beginning had wanted to kidnap me. This was a liminal or transitional world between the natural world and the spiritual one.

The kind old man spoke to me again: "Now that you are going back to your house, take these pants that you have long forgotten here. It was missing these pants that made you so sick and put you in danger of returning to this world where you are still right now. Take them away! Here they are."

Saying this, he lowered some old trousers that remained hanging on one of the forks of his small straw house. I received them from him, and, throwing them over my shoulder, said goodbye to the kind old man. Forgetting those pants had made me sick, according to the old man. It was a symbol of being incomplete. I had something of mine lost or forgotten, which is why my being was affected. Somehow, I did not worry about receiving those pants, because there was no one to stop me, as in the other dimension of the afterlife where I was before. There, my guides prevented me from receiving gifts and food from those who dwell there, as it was the true place of death.

I walked alone through mountains and hollows until I got to the stonework bridge, near the cemetery west of town.

FIGURE 6 Cemetery of Xajla', Jacaltenango, 1982. Photo by the author.

I entered my town and walked alone through its cobbled streets. Very few people passed by, and I greeted those who did, but they seemed not to look at me. They brushed past me as if unaware of my presence.

Then I saw behind me that two men were following me closely. They wanted to surprise me from behind and capture me again. When I saw them I ran, and they did the same to catch up with me. They both looked like the one who had snatched me while I was resting at the foot of the old guava tree. So I started running and running to escape the hands of these kidnappers. But those two men followed me like mad dogs. Then I thought about hiding in my house, and I hurried toward it. They were already catching up with me when another man who came to my defense intercepted them. Those who were chasing me stopped abruptly and I heard what they were saying.

"Why are you so foolish? Why do you keep chasing this poor man?" Thus shouted the one who tried to block their way.

The others, visibly infuriated, yelled back in response: "He hasn't completed his teachings on Sundays! That is his error! We will take him again, by sheer force if we must!"

"Look, don't be reckless. Give up your purpose and leave him alone. And if you hurt him, I will respond." This is how this man who defended me spoke to them; my guides weren't there to explain to me what would happen if I didn't teach on a Sunday. Those who were chasing me were standing there without being able to pass, because the one who protected me seemed stronger than the two combined.

The one who was protecting me spoke to them again, "Did you hear me? Leave him here at his home and don't take it into account on that list you carry."

When my protector finished saying this, my pursuers turned and departed. Then my defender calmly led me to my bed.

Once I got home, I wanted to hide inside a rolled-up duffel in the corner of the house, but my companion stopped me, saying, "You don't have to do that! Be still, those captors won't come back!"

I calmed down being home. But in those moments, I was startled to see many people gathered in the entryway. I did not know why my wife and many of my female relatives were crying loudly. So, I approached a lady to ask her what was happening. But the lady didn't answer, she seemed to be deaf. Or was it that she hadn't heard me? I asked her again louder, almost screaming. She did not answer; she only looked all around her, frightened. Far from answering me, the lady was more scared, and she hastily sat down in the middle of the group of women burning candles in front of the altar.

I entered the house, but no one seemed to see nor hear me. Tears welled up in my eyes from the sadness reigning over the house. Why didn't they look at me the way I looked at them? Why wouldn't they talk to me?

Saddened, I approached someone lying on a table and covered with white sheets. And there, I saw my own eyes open! I was the one lying on the bed, bathed in sweat! Then the voices started to be more real to me. I tried to get up and talk to them, but only managed to move my feet and head, slightly. Seeing me wake up from that unusual dream or almost death, those who were crying turned their tears into joy. Little by little they approached where I was to caress my hands and my face. They couldn't believe what their eyes saw.

They changed my clothes, without my being able to speak yet. I remained dumbstruck, although I did begin to feel a hazy languor, along with the sensation of pain and fatigue in my body. At the same time, an insatiable thirst tormented me, and so I kept drinking water in large quantities. My aching body trembled nonstop, and I still could not believe I was alive, or awake. Was all I saw a terrible dream from the other side? I still felt like I was walking in that mysterious place where I had gone, without knowing now where it was.

Bit by bit, a terrible fatigue took over me, sinking me again into a deep sleep. Not until dawn of the next day did I wake up, but still could not speak. Three days passed, after which I was able to talk a little. To those who came to see me, I told what I had seen, just as those up there had commissioned me. Some believed me and promised to behave better from then on. Others simply listened and did not care much about my story. At least, I wanted to fulfill the order of those who allowed me that macabre trip; tell people that there really is a life beyond the earthly one.

When I regained my strength and was able to walk, I immediately went to Xhepel's house to deliver the message that I had brought from Xiwb'alb'a, the place of death. Luckily, she wanted to receive me and listened to the message I was carrying.

I related what I had seen there in the afterlife where the spirits suffer without measure in the clutches of the Vukub' Q'aquix overseers. I also told her about the suffering of that mare who was ruthlessly tortured back in Xiwb'alb'a. I told her my guides had ordered me to slap the leg of the mare, as a signal for her to believe me. And she did believe me, because, very worried, she checked her thigh to discover the sign. Sure enough, there she discovered a handprint mysteriously etched on her left thigh like a tattoo. She had not realized how or when that mysterious signal from the afterlife appeared. Then she immediately understood that she was on the wrong path, and so she repented. There is no way to return to see, but I am sure that the tortured spirit, or mare, would have also achieved her freedom for this woman who, without knowing, already had her soul suffering prematurely down in Xiwb'alb'a.

For a long time, I continued to tell my afterlife story to people who visited me, because many had interest in knowing if there is life in the great beyond. I told them what I had seen and lived in the company of my wise and kind guides. Those who paid the most attention were the most traditionalist, because during the 1930s there was much concern about losing the teachings of the ancestors. Everyone said we should not lose the customs of the ancestors, since they had shown us the road to follow with the sacred Maya calendar. For their part, the priests and politicians of this decade insisted on eradicating our ancient customs, condemning our religious practices as teachings of the devil. Thus the tradition of the village prayer-leaders was abolished, and I could no longer serve the people as I had proposed. Of course, I kept insisting that it is not religion that solves human problems, but rather living and understanding the moral universe built by our ancestors. The key is respect and reciprocity between Hunab' K'uh, man and nature to live peacefully and without much suffering.

I could never regain my full health, as the disease I suffered continued to weaken my body during the several years I lived after my abduction beyond the grave. Furthermore, the dictators in office continued to trample on the rights of us Indigenous people, plunging us into extreme poverty. I had to live the last years of my life under the dictatorship of then President Jorge Ubico. This tyrant condemned the Indigenous people of Guatemala to forced labor by creating cursed and discriminatory laws such as the Law Against Vagrancy. With this law, the government forced Indigenous people to work on the construction of roads without any payment, as if we were slaves. I imagine these tyrants will also have their place in hell when they die, because they have made so many people suffer who ask for justice. There is not much difference between them and the conquerors and encomenderos who began the destruction of our peoples when they first settled among us.

Finally, I can say that life beyond the grave is a parody of life on earth. If you choose to live with joy and give your body rest without mistreating it, well, you will do the same in the other life. If, on the contrary, you live a disorderly life and make your body suffer, then your soul will also suffer in that other life.

For my ancestors, heaven meant going to revel in a beautiful place under the shade of a gigantic ceiba tree, with all kinds of fruits, honey, and food to enjoy. In other words, a paradise where you suffer no thirst, hunger, or disease.

I am confused, because my belief is still a mixture and I believe that heaven and hell are what one builds or prepares on earth, and the spirit will achieve what one wants to believe will be in the afterlife.

After my vision from beyond the grave, I can affirm that life is like a brief exhalation, and when the spirit escapes from the body at the moment of death, it materializes in an instant like a rippling golden thread, borne on the wind. Upon penetrating the level of the gray or liminal world, it takes its human form, and this is where the true journey to *kamb'al*, the place of death, begins.

EPILOGUE

Kidnapped to the Underworld: The Work in Context

WHEN THE anthropologist Oliver La Farge visited the Maya region during his first expedition from Tulane University in Louisiana in 1925, he was surprised by certain news of great anthropological interest. A neighbor in the city of Comitán, Chiapas, Mexico told him that on the other side of the border in Jacaltenango, Guatemala, people still practiced an ancient Maya ceremony the Indigenous there called Ijom Hab'il or Year Bearer. Motivated by this surprising information, La Farge organized the third expedition from Tulane University to go to western Guatemala. On this expedition (1927), La Farge visited the Cuchumatán mountains and established himself among the Jakaltek Mayas of northwestern Guatemala. In his ethnography *The Year Bearer's People* (1931), La Farge described the intensity with which the people entered into the spiritual world of their ancestors during the Ijom Hab'il ceremony. In other words, La Farge observed that, at the end of the 1920s, the religious tradition of the Jakaltek Mayas remained just as vigorous as in pre-Hispanic times.

In the same book, La Farge mentioned that this ceremony was at that time under attack from Catholic missionaries and civil authorities. The Catholic Church was becoming preoccupied with the persistence of these Indigenous traditions which it thought should already have disappeared. The fact that people in Jacaltenango were still practicing a pre-Hispanic ceremony like Ijom Hab'il showed that the labor of the Catholic missionaries to Christianize the Jakaltek had not been very successful. On some occasions, La Farge was able to persuade the Jacaltenango parish priest that it was important to learn and understand the Indigenous tradition before destroying it, since the Mayas had much to teach westerners. But the missionaries kept pressuring the traditional religious leaders to abandon their supposedly pagan religious practices. According to La Farge (1931), many of those called *chimanes* (shamans) or Maya priests and seers in Jacaltenango were captured and sent to prisons in Huehuetenango or Quetzaltenango in an effort to eradicate the Year Bearer ceremony.

Indigenous beliefs about the great beyond and the kingdom of the dead had been replaced with medieval European and Christian concepts. The underworld, which for the Mayas had been a vague wandering with no eternal rest, became a place of fire and flames. The image of the devil as an evil being with horns and a tail was popularized among the Indigenous by the evangelical Catholic religion. Indigenous people began to adapt themselves to these Western beliefs during the catechization of the early years of Spanish conquest and colonization of America.

Due to the persecution of community political-religious leaders, many Jakaltek who were in the process of Ladinoization allied themselves with priests and civil authorities, pushing the traditionalists to eliminate the Ijom Hab'il ceremony in 1947. Those who wanted to continue serving in matters of religion approached the Catholic Church and began to strengthen another mixed tradition, that of the teacher-singers or *mastrocoros.* This was an effort

* Contraction of the two words maestro, master, and coro, choir or chorus. Also called corista, it was a religious position held by men who could read and write, akin to the ancient role of assistant to the main Maya priest. It was considered a preferred way of giving service to please God.

to continue the ancient tradition of *ahtz'ib*, writers and poets, and *ahb'it*, singers of spiritual themes who acted as chorus leaders. There also existed common singers called *b'itlom*, who sang popular, lay, and profane songs. Among this group are the *nimq'omlom*, or "those of the sacred discourse." They are specialized orators who present offerings to the Creator, utilizing the language of the flowers, or el lenguaje florido. This type of service to the pueblo responded to the "promises" that parents made to Komam Jahaw (God) so that their children would not die from the common epidemics at that time. The Virgin of Candelaria, patron saint of the town, was asked for her intercession so that the sons and daughters (*k'ahole-kutz'ineh*) would grow up safe and sound; and that one day, as adults, they would serve God and their people.

At the beginning of the 20th century, epidemics continued to claim many lives in western Guatemala, and people became greatly concerned about their children's health and future. For this reason, the practice of "spiritual promises" (*nab'eb'al* or *recordatorio*) arose to fulfill the promises made to the Creator to allow daughters and sons to grow up healthy and strong.

This was, then, a pre-Hispanic practice that the Jakaltek Maya continued, especially through the Ijom Hab'il ceremony. Unfortunately, this Ijom Hab'il ceremony, so vividly observed and described by Oliver La Farge (1931), could not continue due to the violent attacks against Maya spiritual guides and prayer leaders. Curiously, this was during the revolutionary government of Juan José Arévalo (1944–1948) when political parties were present in the communities. At that time, the Ladinoized Maya who took the leadership of the political parties considered that the political-religious system of the "cargo" or Ijom Hab'il was unpaid work that constituted forced labor and had to be abolished. With this erroneous interpretation of community service under the Arévalo government's new law against forced labor, the Ijom Hab'il ceremony was totally abolished in 1947. Since then, Maya spirituality and Catholicism have become more and more mixed. Out of this mixture emerged a more syncretic and tolerant Catholicism that is still practiced in the Indigenous communities of Guatemala.

From this violent religious change arises my grandfather's story, vision, or dream, as related in this work. At first, my grandfather Antonio Esteban was a traditional man, although he was also one of the few who could read and write in the community at that time (1920s). Because of his literacy skills, my grandfather could mediate between the Maya people and the few Ladinos or Mestizos who lived in the town. He served the community and also served as a *mastrocoro*, because those who did this work of answering songs of the mass in Latin needed to read the books that were kept in the parish church choir.

My grandfather served as *mastrocoro* for several years and became familiar with the teachings of the catechism and the preachings of the priests.

One day, shortly before the Maya New Year or Ijom Hab'il, my grandfather was visited by the outgoing *alkal txah* or prayer leaders to ask him to become the new authority for the year and serve the people.* As said before, due to the attacks suffered by the traditionalist Maya spiritual guides, it was necessary to put people who could read and write at the head of such a service or position. In this way they could articulate the two cultures with different worldviews. The pueblo thought they needed to have leaders who could direct the political-religious affairs of the people and defend them from external attacks on the traditional culture. People understood that it was necessary to defend the Indigenous cultural tradition, while interacting with the outside world that included the parish priest, who also spoke Spanish.

This service, as everyone knew, was very important and sacred, because it is believed that the human being at birth brings with

---

* This is part of the *cargo* system, the most important form of political-religious service among the Indigenous of Mesoamerica. Those who complete their service go on to become the principales or councilors to the people: the Council of Elders.

his life a mission in the world and that his first promise of life is to "serve God, serve your people and serve your community." According to *Popol Vuh*, human beings should be grateful for the life, health, and intelligence that they have received from the Creator and Maker. This is how the first created fathers and mothers gave thanks to the Creator saying, "¡En verdad os damos gracias, dos y tres veces! Hemos sido creados, se nos ha dado una boca y una cara y podemos hablar, oír, pensar y caminar . . . Les damos gracias, pues, por habernos creado ¡oh Creador y Formador!" (Recinos 1978, 101; We truly thank you, two and three times! We have been created, we have been given a mouth and a face and we can speak, hear, think and walk . . . We thank you, then, for having created us, oh Creator and Maker!). The promise of service to the Creator in gratitude for life was thus an ancient and practical concept among the Mayas.

When my grandfather was asked to serve the town with the *alkal txah cargo*, he rejected such service, arguing that he was very poor and had spent much of his time serving in the church as a *mastrocoro*. It was time to dedicate himself a little to his family and try to lift them out of the extreme poverty that total community service led to. In other words, those who served the people according to the *cargo* system ended up very poor at the end of their year of community service. They could not plant their milpa and depended on products from the communal milpa, cultivated by all to sustain those with a sacred cargo.

My grandfather replied that he had already served on other occasions and that it was advisable to find another suitable person for that service. It had become customary to keep appointing the same leaders, since few Indigenous people knew how to read or write. My grandfather flatly rejected the proposal to serve again as *alkal txah*, or prayer leader.

But the Indigenous tradition was strict regarding the sacred charge of *alkal txah*. It was a service to God that could not be refused in any way. Anyone who disobeyed and rejected a service of this nature was rejecting the norm of reciprocity that must exist between the Creator, humans, and nature. In other words, to refuse to serve in a sacred office was, to some extent, to deny his health and to reject the blessings of the Creator, putting his life at risk and without protection. Everyone knew, then, that refusing to serve in this sacred and communal office could be disastrous for those who rejected it.

My mother says that shortly after rejecting the sacred service to the pueblo, my grandfather suddenly fell ill. A rare disease, or what in this context is called *naj hustisya* (divine justice) kept him weak, and he fell into bed for a long time.

My mother remembers well that moment when my grandfather was crazy and, even though the family called the best healers in town, nobody really knew what was wrong with him. Everyone believed that he was paying for his sin of rejecting the sacred traditions of the people. There he lay ill for some years until he had this dream, vision, or near-death experience that I have related here.

This story is relevant because it shows us the deep religiosity of the Indigenous peoples of Guatemala and the American continent. In addition, we can affirm that there are many similarities between the Catholic religion and Maya spirituality, as documented by the early missionaries who arrived during and after the Spanish invasion of these lands. Of course, the figurative idea of hell is different from that of the Maya, since the "sea of fire," or hell, and the very image of the devil are medieval representations that have persisted to explain the dogmas of faith. My grandfather experienced this transformation and went from being a traditional Maya to practicing the creed of the Catholic Church as a choirmaster. So this dream, or vision, of my grandfather shows us the changes in the abstract conceptions that Indigenous peoples have about the eternal values we call heaven and hell.

REFERENCES

La Farge, Oliver, and Douglas Byers. 1931. *The Year Bearer's People*. Middle American Research Series 3. New Orleans: The Tulane University of Louisiana.

Montejo, Victor D. 2021. Entre dos Mundos: Una Memoria. Guatemala: Editorial Piedra Santa.

Recinos, Adrián. 1978. El *Popol Vuh*: Las antiguas historias del Quiché. México City: Época.

GLOSSARY

Ah-b'it: Singers, or people of the song.

Ah-tz'ib': One having knowledge of letters and writing, Maya scribe.

Alkal txah or alcalde rezador: Prayer maker, a sacred position in the ancient Maya tradition.

Capixhay: Traditional wool coat.

Chichimit: Character in the dance of Cortés, Chichimec warrior.

Chilam B'alam: The sage and seer, jaguar priest.

Cusha: Locally distilled liquor made from brown sugar and other ingredients.

Güaro: Cane liquor.

Hunab' K'uh: The One True God. According to the Mayas.

Ijom Hab'il: ancestral Maya ceremony of the Year Bearer or Celebration of the Maya New Year. Ijom: bearer, and Hab'il: year in Jakaltek Maya (popb'alti').

Kamb'al: The place of death, or where the dead reside.

Komam Jahaw: Our Father and Lord of Our Life. In reference to God.

Ladinizado: Process of change of identity, from Indigenous to Ladino or Mestizo.

Marimba: Percussion instrument made of wood. National symbol of Guatemala.

Marimbista: Person who plays marimba.

Mastrocoro (Maestro de coro): Specialists in Latin responses during mass. This group of singers would occupy the church's choir section. It was a prestigious religious office among the Jakaltek.

Mayab': The region or territory of Mesoamerica where the Maya civilization developed.

Nab'eb'al: Spiritual Promises or "reminder" (recordatorio) of the promises made to the Creator to grant that daughters and sons would grow healthy and strong.

Naj hustisya: Divinely originating punishment for disobeying norms of conduct according to Maya spirituality.

Polacos: Regionalism, a form of saying "local police."

Popol Vuh: Sacred book of the Mayas.

Pozol: Drink made from corn dough, sometimes with cocoa.

Tanhb'al mul: Purgatory, or the place of expiation for guilt and sin.

Txikilah: Or cempasúchil, yellow colored flower known as the flower of the dead. They bloom in November and serve to decorate the graves of the dead.

Tx'ojye-swi': Prostitute or woman of immoral life.

Uwes, wes: Jakaltek term to denominate strangers, Ladinos or the non-Indigenous.

Vukub' Q'aquix: (Seven Fires). Character from *Popol Vuh* who boasted of being the sun, the moon and the one who incited wars and conquests. Similar to Lucifer according to Christian tradition.

Xajla': Ancient Maya name of the pueblo of Jacaltenango.

Xiwb'alb'a or Xibalba: The place of fear and trials.

ABOUT THE AUTHOR AND TRANSLATOR

Victor Montejo is a professor emeritus of Native American studies at University of California, Davis, and a nationally and internationally recognized author. His major publications include *Testimony: Death of a Guatemalan Village* (1987), *Voices from Exile: Violence and Survival in Modern Maya History* (1999), *Maya Intellectual Renaissance: Critical Essays on Identity, Representation, and Leadership* (2003), *Popol Vuh: Sacred Book of the Mayas* (1999), *El Q'anil: Man of Lightning* (2002), *Entre dos Mundos (Memoria)* (2021), and *Mayalogue: An Interactionist Theory of Indigenous Cultures* (2021).

Sean S. Sell is co-editor and translator of *Chiapas Maya Awakening: Contemporary Poems and Short Stories* and translator of *Ch'ayemal nich'nabiletik / Los hijos errantes / The Errant Children: A Trilingual Edition*. His work has also been published in the *Latin Americanist*, the *Quiet Corner Interdisciplinary Journal*, and *TRANSMODERNITY: Journal of Peripheral Cultural Production of the Luso-Hispanic World*. Sell has a PhD in comparative literature from the University of California, Davis, where he currently a professor.